W9-CLX-745

THE LEARNING COMPANY

THE LEARNING COMPANY

A strategy for sustainable development

Mike Pedler
John Burgoyne
Tom Boydell

McGRAW-HILL BOOK COMPANY

London · New York · St Louis · San Francisco · Auckland · Bogotá · Caracas
Lisbon · Madrid · Mexico · Milan · Montreal · New Delhi · Panama
Paris · San Juan · São Paulo · Singapore · Sydney · Tokyo · Toronto

Published by
McGRAW-HILL Book Company Europe
Shoppenhangers Road, Maidenhead, Berkshire SL6 2QL, England
Telephone 01628 23432
Fax 01628 770224

British Library Cataloguing in Publication Data
Pedler, Mike
  The learning company.
  1. Management. Training
  I. Title II. Burgoyne, John III. Boydell, Thomas
  658.407124

  ISBN 0-07-707479-3

Library of Congress Cataloging-in-Publication Data
Pedler, Mike
    The learning company : a strategy for sustainable development
  Mike Pedler, John Burgoyne, Tom Boydell.
    p. cm.
    Includes bibliographical references.
    ISBN 0-07-707479-3
    1. Organizational change. I. Burgoyne, John (John G.)
  II. Boydell, Tom. III. Title.
  HD58.8.P43   1991
  658.4´063–dc20   91-13390

78CL94

Typeset by BookEns Limited, Baldock, Herts.
and printed and bound in Great Britain by Clays Ltd, St Ives plc

Printed on permanent paper in compliance with the ISO Standard 9706

Contents

The authors

Mike Pedler is well known for his work in management development, particularly in person-centred or self-developmental approaches. His current work is chiefly concerned with the ideas of organizational learning. Prior to becoming an independent consultant, he worked for Procter & Gamble, British Steel, the Workers' Educational Association, and Sheffield Polytechnic. He is editor of *Management Education & Development*, the journal of the Association of Management Education and Development, and co-author, with David Megginson, of *Self-Development: A Facilitator's Guide*, published by McGraw-Hill in 1991 as part of the McGraw-Hill Training Series.

Tom Boydell is a director of Transform (Individual and Organizational Development) UK Ltd. He is also well known for his work in management development and is currently interested in Total Quality Management. Previous posts include training advisor for the Iron & Steel Industry Training Board and a principal lecturer at Sheffield City Polytechnic.

John Burgoyne has spent 17 years at the University of Lancaster, as research director and then professor and head of department of the Centre for the Study of Management Learning. Over this time he has established a high reputation for his work in management thinking. His initial training was in psychology and he has a PhD from the Manchester Business School, where he was also a lecturer.

All three authors have published numerous articles and books. They are the co-authors of **A manager's guide to self-development** and **Self-development in organizations**, published by McGraw-Hill.

Preface

We first began working together in 1976 and have developed our relationship through collaborating on books, conferences, study groups and each other's programmes. In many ways the business end of the partnership owes its longevity to the idea of self-development, a fringe idea of the 1960s and 1970s that has been absorbed into mainstream thought.

While continuing to harvest the benefits of self-development, we were becoming aware that it was not enough. Empowering individuals within hierarchical, restrictive organizations was insufficient, even hazardous for those individuals. We needed to go further, to embrace both the individual and the organization. From the mid-1980s we were looking for a new idea. We were each pursuing interests in new fields: Tom was getting excited by Total Quality Management (TQM), Mike was working on small business and community development and John was thinking about management development policy, and of the whole business of developing people, as a moral craft. A key development was a speech in early 1986 made by Geoffrey Holland, then Director of the Manpower Services Commission, calling for a new management development initiative in the UK:

> If we are to survive – individually or as companies, or as a country – we must create a tradition of 'learning companies'. Every company must be a 'learning company'.[1]

Here was new language – Learning Company – not the Learning Organization or Learning System of literature or Learning Community, a term used by one of the adult learning theorists. 'Learning Company' had a very good ring to it. Geoffrey Holland didn't know where he'd got the term from and encouraged us to do some research. Almost immediately we made the term Learning Company an idea into which we began to put our individual and collective energies.

This book is one of the outcomes of that work. In the years that have passed since we first began thinking about it, the idea of the Learning Company has not diminished in its brilliance. Despite the efforts, it often seems no nearer in terms of realization, yet it continues to excite imaginations and encourage ambitions. This book is a contribution towards a continuing quest. It does not purport to be a definitive picture but it does set out to encourage people to take charge in company with others not just to earn but to learn together.

In this book we hope you will find some intriguing ideas, some pointers to appropriate methods and some useful tools that you can use right away. This is not a book to be read right through at one sitting, but to be ransacked, referred to, browsed over and, hopefully, encouraged and inspired by. More like a collection of short stories than a novel, it does not attempt completeness, it has no beginning, no middle, no end. It is an early chart of some new territory for us and we hope it encourages you to start the journey and thereby make a better map.

REFERENCES

1.   Holland, G., *Excellence in Industry: Developing Managers – A New Approach*, speech given at the Dorchester Hotel, London, 11 February 1986, Manpower Services Commission (1986).

1. The idea of the Learning Company

This book is for people who believe that there is massive underdeveloped potential in our organizations *and* who want to set about releasing it. The resulting energy can transform us as individuals and change the way we do things together – if we dare and if we have the skills to manage this daring process.

The Learning Company is a vision of what might be possible. It is not brought about simply by training individuals; it can only happen as a result of *learning at the whole organization level*:

> A Learning Company is an organization that facilitates the learning of all its members *and* continuously transforms itself.

def

This is the dream – that we can design and create organizations which are capable of adapting, changing, developing and transforming themselves in response to the needs, wishes and aspirations of people, inside and outside. Such companies will always be realizing their assets without predatory takeovers; they will be able to flex without hiring a new Top Man; they will be able to avoid the sudden and massive restructurings that happen after years of not noticing the signals.

wrong!
organism

We use the term 'Learning Company' rather than 'Learning Organization' because we think it more convivial. 'Organization' is a mechanical sort of word, sounding somewhat abstract and lifeless, and the prospect of dealing with it is perhaps intimidating. 'Company', on the other hand, is one of our oldest words for a group of people engaged in a joint enterprise. In everyday terms we 'accompany' others and talk of doing things 'in company'. So we use the word 'company' for any collective endeavour and not to identify or give preference to a particular legal form or ownership pattern.

?

 # B. S. resm

Who, then, are our companions – the members of the Learning Company – and what do we mean by '. . . continuously transforms itself'? These questions are explored in depth in the following chapters. Incidentally, we take a wide view of who the 'members' are – employees, owners, customers, suppliers, neighbours, the environment and even competitors in some cases.

2 The Learning Company

Creating the Learning Company is easier said than done. While there is no short-age of theories as to how it may be done, most of them come without examples. We can't take you out to visit a Learning Company or bring in a blueprint of what worked elsewhere – it's not like that. The magic of the Learning Company has to be realized from within. The key word is 'transformation' – a radical change in the form and character of what is already there.

There are plenty of ideas in this book to try out in your company. We call these ideas Glimpses of the Learning Company and you will find 101 of them in the pages that follow. These Glimpses show just some of the possibilities and are taken from a wide variety of organizations. There is no set path to follow the vision of the Learning Company; but there are lots of points where you can take your first step.

An old dream?

The literature relevant to the Learning Company is voluminous. The terms 'Learning Company' or 'Learning Organization' are relatively recent but the idea has been around for a long time. The struggle for compatibility between personal growth and organized human relationships goes back at least to Moses. Since the 1950s, the development of systems thinking, and particularly the socio-technical systems view of organizations, are probably most responsible for allowing us to imagine organizations as organisms – as living things – that can therefore, among other things, learn.

The writings of Gregory Bateson[1] on types of learning, especially his theory of 'deutero-learning', which concerns learning to learn, have been influential. John Gardner in 1963[2] used the term 'self-renewal' and Gordon Lippitt[3] 'organization renewal' in 1969, to capture this living, learning quality they sought. The term 'learning system' was brought into the mainstream by Donald Schon[4] in his 1970 Reith Lectures and the same term is used by Reg Revans[5] in the UK in 1969. Much of the literature is focused on the 'organization development' movement that has change as a central concern though it is often expressed rather too sys-tematically as 'planned organizational change'.

The recent interest in the Learning Company perhaps begins with Argyris and Schon's *Organizational Learning*.[6] The idea was picked up but not developed by Peters and Waterman when they said, 'The excellent companies are learning organizations'.[7] Revans[5] and Garratt[8] have made it the prime responsibility of company directors and senior managers, Attwood and Beer[9] have applied it to the Health Service, Holly and Southworth[10] to schools and in our earlier research[11] we have described it as the theme most likely to preoccupy managers in the coming years.

Here ends the history lesson. It was important to include it to illustrate that the

Learning Company is not a new dream, but is still a topical one. The aim of this book is to help you to take courage and make a start. To act and to learn from acting, for action alone is not enough. Action in the Learning Company always has two purposes:

- to resolve the immediate problem;
- to learn from that process.

The emphasis in this book is upon managerial action as experiment rather than as the 'right answer'. The history of managing is littered with the remains of yesterday's 'right answers' – scientific management, theories X and Y, Blake's Grid, MbO, Quality Circles, the search for excellence and so on. So, where are they now and what did we learn from these experiments?

We are all sometimes tempted by the promise of the 'quick fix'. Each of the methods listed above contain good ideas, but ideas bought and sold as right answers quickly become empty techniques and the life goes out of them. We know in our hearts that there are no easy answers to the complex problems of organizing work, so how can we get beyond the quick fix mentality?

Only by learning, which increases our confidence and empowers us to enquiry, action and further learning. If ideas, such as briefing groups or profit centres, can be seen as experiments rather than solutions then we can learn from them. The company that can learn from experience of trying out new ways of operating will have a massive advantage over one that does not.

Learning is the key to survival and development for the companies of the 1990s. In the last 20 years we have learned a lot about helping individuals to learn; now the challenge is to understand and master the art of corporate learning. This book is written as part of that quest.

How do companies come to be the way they are?

When we think about what companies are like, why they are the way they are and what is involved in their change and evolution, we come up with a number of different perspectives. We find three of these particularly helpful.

- Ideas   Companies are first a product of the visions and images that their founders sought to create, which are passed on through history and mythology and which succeeding generations try to recreate. These are the idea of building the world's best mousetrap, to be 'excellent', to realize a concept of a holding company portfolio of autonomous operating units, a clever matrix structure or, indeed, our own working list of the characteristics of a Learning Company. In the beginning is the idea – nothing starts without it – and a company can be anything its members design and plan it to be: provided that they can put this into practice.

- Life stage   Are they new, infant, pioneering, established, mature, trying to change long-established customs and ways of doing things, winding up (or down), passing on resources, assets and expertise to new ventures and partnerships? Although companies can be given new life, rather like George Washington's axe in the American museum that has had three new heads and six new handles since he used it, perhaps a company needs to be of a form and behaviour appropriate to its age or stage. In these terms it will be a poor learner if it tries to hold back from, or run ahead of, its 'natural' stage of development.

- Era   Companies are shaped by, and fit in with, the economic and cultural contexts in which they exist. As a general point this is easy to accept, but to be specific in terms of how this works is very difficult. The notion of era is partly to do with the broad macroeconomic phases of pre-industrial, industrial, post-industrial and also the locally predominant type of economic activity, e.g., primary, secondary, tertiary. These macropatterns progress in different forms and on different time scales depending on location. For example, a hi-tech company in California operates in a different era from an agricultural business in a poor country. However, they are increasingly part of the same 'global village' and a computer-controlled irrigation project could be a good and feasible joint venture. This perspective is even further complicated by the post-modern thesis that we are entering the era that marks the end of era-style development. 'Progress' as such does not exist and development is multi-directional and paradoxical. Despite these difficulties, the notion of era and how we fit in with it, is a factor that makes our company what it is today.

Each of these three perspectives offers something to the way we think about how companies come to be the way they are and what form their development may take. In this book we try to work with all three, although our concern with the *idea* of the Learning Company shows a special allegiance to the force of ideas in shaping practice. We believe that it is possible to choose ideas, apply them and thereby shape the company, but we think that it is wise to do this with an awareness of, and a sensitivity to, the wider forces of life-phase and era.

This trilogy of ideas, phases and eras provides some of the structure of this book. In Chapter 2 we develop the argument that the Learning Company is an idea for the present; that its era has come. Chapter 3 offers a working framework of the idea so that any given company can be viewed from this perspective as the beginnings of the process of becoming a Learning Company.

In Chapter 4 we suggest that a company biography approach can give an interpretation of the appropriate form for the current phase of your company organization. As in the previous chapter, a framework is offered through which any company can be viewed in order to clarify the choices available at this stage of its life. Chapter 5 invites you to go in for some 'era spotting', to engage in a little speculation about the wider context in which your company operates. What's your reading of this context and how might a Learning Company strategy fit in?

Having decided that a Learning Company strategy is part of the future for your company, Chapter 6 offers some starting points for this. In our view there is no one right point to start, but a number of different possibilities do present themselves. Whichever point is chosen, the holistic nature of the idea suggests that, like a string bag, all aspects of the company are eventually connected.

In Chapter 7 we share our incomplete vision through 101 Glimpses of the Learning Company. These are down-to-earth and specific examples of what some companies are doing that can be seen as part of this idea. These are not case studies of Learning Companies, for none such exist, but possibilities, fragments and facets of this exciting idea. We chose the word 'glimpse' to capture these partial visions and also to make it clear that while no one has got it right, many companies are trying interesting and valuable experiments. From these glimpses we hope you will be able to create your own vision for your company.

REFERENCES

1. Bateson, G., *Steps to an Ecology of Mind*, Paladin (1973).
2. Gardner, J. W., *Self-renewal: The Individual and the Innovative Society*, Harper & Row (1963).
3. Lippitt, G. L., *Organization Renewal*, Appleton-Century-Crofts (1969).
4. Schon, D. A., *Beyond the Stable State*, Random House (1971).
5. Revans, R. W., 'The Enterprise as a Learning System' in R. W. Revans *The Origins and Growth of Action Learning*, Chartwell-Bratt (1982).
6. Argyris, C. and D. A. Schon, *Organizational Learning: A Theory in Action Perspective*, Addison-Wesley (1978).
7. Peters, T. J. and R. H. Waterman, *In Search of Excellence*, Harper & Row (1982).
8. Garratt, R., *The Learning Organization*, Fontana (1987).
9. Attwood, M. and N. Beer, 'Development of a Learning Organization' in *Management Education and Development*, 19(3) pages 201–214, (1988).
10. Holly, P., and G. Southworth, *The Developing School*, Falmer Press (1989).
11. Pedler, M., T. Boydell and J. Burgoyne, *Learning Company Project Report*, Manpower Services Commission (May 1988).

2. Why is the idea of the Learning Company relevant now?

In Chapter 1 we saw how the current state of a company at any one time is the result of three forces: the idea behind it; the phase of its development; and the era it is in. Although these three perspectives are in principle independent, in practice they may well be linked.

Organizational phases, or, the evolution of organizations

Let us start by looking at the phases of organizational development.

Ronnie Lessem[1] makes a particularly thorough exploration of this concept, building on earlier ideas of Lievegoed.[2] In summary, Lessem concludes that organizations progress through four phases or stages.

Primal Phase: the pioneer organization

This is when the organization is formed around an individual or small group – the pioneer. Pioneers have some product or service that they want to produce and sell so they employ people to help with this production and selling. All the sense of energy, drive and direction comes from this pioneer, who remains fully in touch with all employees and, even more importantly, with the customers.

Systems and procedures are kept to the absolute minimum necessary for production, selling and distribution. These systems tend to be very informal with procedures, rules, guidelines and so on not being written down, but kept in the heads of key personnel – who tend to muck in, do whatever is necessary and take turns at a range of activities. Specialization is rather rare. Energy, enthusiasm and loyalty are high – generated by the charismatic personality of the pioneer. The structure is either extremely flat as in Figure 2.1 or like a spider in a web – the pioneer being

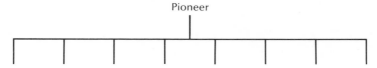

Figure 2.1 Flat early company structure

in the middle of the web, immediately aware of anything that happens anywhere else (Figure 2.2).

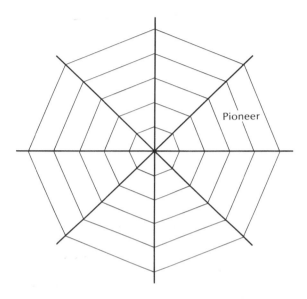

Figure 2.2 Web-like early company structure

Given that organizations virtually always start off in pioneering mode, what happens next?

Some, of course, remain that way for a long time – although eventually they often come to grief when the orginal pioneer dies, retires or simply moves on into some other sphere of interest, leaving an unsurvivable vacuum behind them.

Rational Phase: the differentiated organization

Very often the very success of the primal organization leads to a developmental crisis.

As time proceeds, and the organization grows, the informal, energetic ways of working begin to break down. It's no longer feasible to rely on them for managing larger, complex situations. We have reached what Lievegoed[2] terms the crisis of the 'over-ripe pioneer'. We need to analyse and record our processes, so that they can be systematically improved and newcomers trained. We need specialists to handle particular functions, such as finance, marketing, personnel (hence Lievegoed's use of the term 'differentiated'). Now, therefore, the organization enters the rational or scientific phase.

This is where we find order, rationality, formality, specialization. The world of F. W. Taylor,[3] Weber,[4] Koontz and O'Donnell,[5] Peter Drucker.[6]

In its classical form, this is the phase of the organization chart or 'organigram' (Figure 2.3):

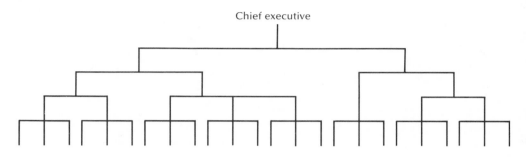

Figure 2.3 An organigram

The bureaucratic crisis

At first, the rationality and order brought to the organization by moving into the Rational Phase usually prove highly beneficial – order replaces chaos, profession-alism replaces energetic amateurism. However, therein lies not only the resolution of the previous crisis, but also the seeds of the next one for while the 'amateurs' of the previous phase, inspired by the actual pioneer, were indeed energetic, enthu-siastic, loyal, committed, the specialists of the rational phase are much less so. Their commitment tends to be to their professional specialism, not the organization. The formal, hierarchical structure, too, gradually generates its own problems of lack of concern for the whole, internal tension, competition and conflict, difficulty or indeed impossibility of good communication and lack of identification with the organization, or, conversely, an unhealthy dependence on it for everything – the 'from the cradle to the grave' mentality of some paternalistic companies (not, be it noted, maternalistic).

At the same time, the energy and attention focused inwards on building up systems and structures turns the attention away from the customer. The organization becomes increasingly out of touch with the real wishes of external stakeholders (although inordinate effort and short-term thinking often go into keeping 'owners' happy, be this reflected in high share prices or toeing the line of party political dogma). Gradually, therefore, the rational organization becomes strangled by its own web of rationality. It becomes an out-of-touch bureaucracy.

The first level of response to this crisis is to try to loosen things up a bit, to break some of the formality, to improve communications, to redirect attention out-wards. Hence we find reorganizations, whether these be mere shuffling of the pieces of the familiar hierarchy, or possibly some form, of matrix management (Figure 2.4) where 'horizontal' temporary project teams supplement the original vertical authority relationships.

Figure 2.4 Matrix management

Here, too, there is often an emphasis on teamwork training, team briefings, resolving conficts between groups, closing down specialist service functions, sub-contracting these out, and often sudden bursts of energy into customer care programmes.

This is only a temporary solution, however. Indeed, it is not a resolution of the crisis. Lessem[1] suggests that Peters and Waterman's[7] ideals are an attempt to go back to the basics of the pioneer phase. Evolution, though, by its very nature, cannot work backwards; in the long-term we have to move forwards.

Another temporary solution is often to lessen the alienation felt by many – if not by most – members of an out-of-touch bureaucracy by bringing in opportunities for self-development, through groups, action-learning sets, special courses, resource centres and the like. Here again, although this may be a step in the right direction, it is not enough. Such opportunities are rarely, if ever, made available to all members and the self-development tends to be self-ish, that is, it is aimed inwards at my 'self', for my own purposes. It has little to do with the organization's goals or with meeting the needs of others.

Another quite different distortion of self-development can be found in extreme laissez-faireism: if you want to learn or develop, do it yourself.

However, although neither of these two different ways of responding to the bureaucratic crisis can prove of long-term value in themselves, they are both helpful = necessary perhaps – in preparing for the next true phase.

Developmental Phase: the integrated organization

'The integrated organization' is Lievegoed's[2] term for this phase and it gives a good indication of one of the main characteristics that we find here. Now we begin to see real signs of integration between all sorts of people, functions and ideas that were previously seen as separate:

function A	[with]	function B
team X	[with]	team Y
process P	[with]	process Q
manager	[with]	managed
this company	[with]	our customers
this company	[with]	our suppliers
this company	[with]	our owners
this company	[with]	our environment
this company	[with]	our competitors
me	[with]	you
women	[with]	men
black	[with]	white
idea	[with]	deed
policy	[with]	practice
vision	[with]	action
values	[with]	processes
intention	[with]	achievement

[and vice versa.]

Whereas we know quite a lot about the differentiated organization and a certain amount about the pioneer, we know rather little about the form of this integration. We are still experimenting and various suggestions have been made, such as Lievegoed's[2] clover leaf, Handy's[8] shamrock or, in this book, the four eights model, as discussed in the next chapter. However, it's not easy to turn these into practice – to make deeds of these ideas – although this book gives glimpses of how we might start to do so.

It is in this phase, then, that we find the Learning Company as we define it, (that's not to say, of course, that many of the ideas and practices associated with the Learning Company cannot be applied at an earlier phase of development, but they may well need modifying in the light of the company's evolutionary position and Chapter 4 looks specifically at this – as a rather obvious example, a company in the pioneer phase, with very few systems and procedures, will need to tackle information in a different way than would a stuck bureaucracy).

This is also the phase of Total Quality Management (TQM), particularly the approach taken by Deming.[9] His proposed organizational form is being put into practice in a number of organizations. It shows a flow through a chain of suppliers and customers, as we can see in Figure 2.5.

Here, too, as we move towards a wider scale of integration we start to be con-

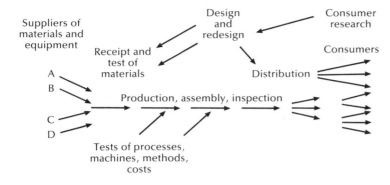

Suppliers of
materials and
equipment

Design
and
redesign

Consumer
research

Receipt and
test of
materials

Consumers

A

B

Production, assembly, inspection

Distribution

C

D

Tests of processes,
machines, methods,
costs

Figure 2.5 Deming's form for organizations

fronted with issues of ethics and morality. So working on the ethical organization is another way into exploring the integrated phase.

Finally we come to an even greater level – or is it depth – of integration, that of matter and spirit. In physics this has long been recognized – that apparently solid matter is actually made up of invisible energy patterns – but in the world of organizations this view has yet to become widely recognized, although writers such as Harrison Owen[10] (and the 'organization transformation' school) and Ronnie Lessem[1] have done a lot to bring it into focus. Indeed, Lessem sees this as the next phase, which he calls 'metaphysical'. Rich and complex though the phases be, underpinning each lie some very simple ideas, which may be summarized as shown in Table 2.1.

As an organization develops, a new idea becomes manifest through it. Conversely, in order to develop, an organization requires that a new idea be brought in.

It will be seen that, after a period of time, a positive idea will gradually become distorted, polluted or simply over-the-top, too much of a good thing. The dynamic excitement of 'excellence' and 'winning' become distorted into 'chaos' and 'tough luck on losers'. 'Order' and 'structure' become 'rigidity' and 'compartmentalization'. These are what we mean by 'the double' of the original idea, they are distorted forms of something good. In fact, there seems to be a natural process at work here – perhaps linked to the physicists' concept of entropy. Just as there is a natural tendency in the physical world to disorder and decay, so is there a natural tendency for a good idea to become distorted, applied inappropriately or in excess, for the idea to deteriorate, into its double.

Although this is unfortunate in one sense, it is important to recognize it as an essential aspect of evolution. For it is when the double gets the upper hand that

Phase	Idea	Distorted form of idea (double)	Transformational need
Primal, pioneer	Excellence, winning	Chaos, survival of the fittest (rest go to the wall)	Order, rationality
Rational, differentiated	Order, structure, systematic specialization, growing while remaining stable	Rigidity, compartmentalization, conflict, the established company and/or out-of-touch – the wilderness company	Movement, shake-up, life
Later rational, differentiated	Shake-up, bring movement, improve communication and/ or self-development	Flavour of the month, quick fix, keep your head down and it will go away, self-ish, elitist, used as excuse to do nothing for employees – 'pull yourself up by your bootstraps'	Integration, purpose, meaning, integration, purpose, meaning
Developmental, integrated	Unity, systemic, meaning, purpose, ethics, cooperating, morality, ecology	Purely material	Matter and spirit
Metaphysical, spiritual	Matter and spirit	Attachment to negative forces?	?

Table 2.1   The underlying principles behind the phases, or, the evolution of the idea of organizations

we arrive at the threshold for our next developmental step – when we need a new idea. This is why we will never actually 'get there', we will never get things fully sorted out, for once we solve one problem or issue, another will emerge, the seeds of which have been sown by our previous solution. So we need a further resolution of the new problem. In general terms we can depict this never-ending process as shown in Figure 2.6.

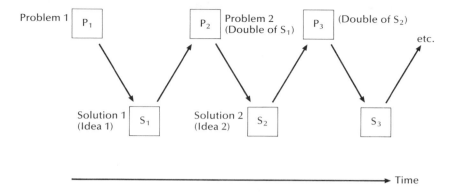

Figure 2.6 The problem-solving process

This is both good news and bad news: bad in that it means we'll always be looking ahead for what new problem will be coming our way; good for the same reason.

Ideas, then, emerge over a period of time. Let's now look at how this has actually worked out in the field of training and development in organizations.

The evolution of training and development

We have to take an arbitrary starting point, which in this case will be post-war Britain (note that time must also include space – 'where' as well as 'when').

Systematic training

After the Second World War there was a need for greater productivity. Various studies and investigations concluded that a major reason for our low productivity compared with that of the USA was lack of skilled workers. The idea of the time being order, planning and so on, the solution was systematic training. Companies were exhorted to try harder but, it was felt, with little success, so eventually a Tory Government passed, and a Labour Government implemented, the Industrial Training Act 1964.

This, then, led to the heyday of systematic training. Based primarily on Rational Phase ideas, it led, by way of best practice, to job descriptions, job specifications, careful identification of training needs, job analysis, behavioural objectives, programme planning and systematic evaluation.[11]

What happened next? If systematic training was S_1, what was P_2? (See Figure 2.7)

As was to be expected, P_2 arose out of the assumptions of S_1. The outcomes of planned training were not consistent, predictable. Jobs cannot be split into micro-skills and put together again. Most, such as managing, require discretionary, not

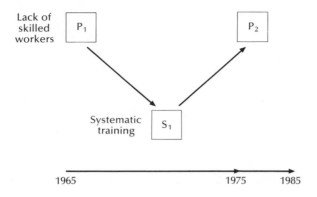

Figure 2.7 The evolution of systematic training

to say artistic abilities (though even now in the 1990s the Management Competencies Movement is making this same S_1-level assumption). People become alienated when treated as measurable, mouldable, purposeless units – especially when the basis for measurement is in any case flawed – and when their essential differences and diversity (sex, race, class and many more) that make up their real being are ignored or, worse, devalued, they become angry.

So at P_2 we have complex structures of training specialists and experts leading to alienated, angry people, equipped with a whole range of micro-skills that don't seem to have much effect when applied at work (the 'transfer of training' problem that was much discussed in journals in the late 1970s).

Three responses to P_2

At this point in time the picture gets a bit more complex and we can depict at least three responses to this crisis – three distinct versions of S_2.

The first in the mid-1970s, was the emergence of Organization Development (OD) as a body of knowledge and practice. It fitted in perfectly with the 'shake-up, improve communication' approach to tackling problems of bureaucracy. It also sowed seeds – at least in the minds of its practitioners, if not its clients – that would start to take root later, in the late 1980s and early 1990s.

The second reaction in the late 1970s and early 1980s might almost be seen as anti-organization. The company now tended to be seen as something that just mucked up peoples' lives and their development. As a counterbalance, self-development methods and approaches began to be used[12] and, naturally enough, these perfectly matched the second approach to transforming bureaucracy.

The third reaction in the early 1980s, triggered by Peters and Waterman, was the pursuit of excellence. In effect, this was saying 'look, we're tired of all this bureau-cracy, let's scrap it and get back to basics'. As already described, Lessem sees this, at its simplest, as a first class exploration of the primal or pioneer phase of organi-zation development that, until now, had not been studied or written about in much depth. None the less, the whole excellence school – based though it is on the notion of *winning* (and hence losing) and thus not in tune with the *win:win* partnership philosophy of the integrated phase – does have some forward pointers as well. For example, it contains a huge element of the 'liven things up, shake it about, improve communications' strategy for tackling bureaucracy.

So, by the mid to late 1980s, current thinking revolved around three points:

- Organization Development, where P_3 was that all this loosening up, working on style, improving communications and the like still didn't seem to be getting anybody anywhere and made them a bit cynical about all these quick fix solutions and flavours of the month. (In one major utility company in the UK there were at one time 13 different company-wide change programmes, each with its championing director, each competing for resources, each getting in the way of the other 12.)
- self-development and action learning, which might have been very beneficial for the personal growth of a rather limited number of the fortunate few, but often did not move the whole company forward and was sometimes used as an excuse to provide no development opportunities at all.
- pursuing excellence, which injected terrific energy and excitement but again didn't really move anybody on (see Figure 2.8).

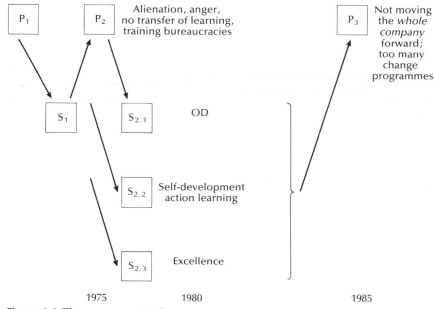

Figure 2.8 The responses to P_2

The late 1980s and early 1990s

From the field of training and development there have been two main streams of response to this. Out of OD came Organizational Transformation (OT) and from self-development and action-learning came the Learning Company.

The name most associated with OT is that of Harrison Owen. In fact, he appears to define transformation in the way we use the word development – that is, to move from one phase of existence to another completely different one. The example he uses is that of the caterpillar turning into a butterfly.

In that sense, OT describes a company moving from pioneer to rational phase or from rational to integrated. Owen himself is very clear on this point. OT is primarily a process, not an end state. He goes on to say, however, that there may be a final phase beyond which we cannot go and that in this condition the company might be said to be fully transformed – 'completion has occurred'.[10] He goes into some detail about how we might move towards this ultimate phase, which he terms the 'Inspired Organization'. The body of practice known as OT tends to focus specifically on this final phase. In our terms, it is therefore clearly a version of S_3.

The other version of S_3 comes from the worlds of self-development and action learning (see Figure 2.9). It suggests that just as individuals learn, so may organizations. This is the time of the Learning Company, as described in Chapter 3.

Summary

We have seen, then, that the Learning Company is here, in the *time-space era* of the early 1990s in the UK. This is because the *ideas* of organization, training and development and of quality management, have evolved to that point. It's no coincidence that an increasing number of organizations are faced with the true bureaucratic crisis *phase in their development,* such that the Learning Company is needed.

REFERENCES

1. Lessem, R., *Global Management Principles,* Prentice-Hall (1989).
2. Lievegoed, B., *The Developing Organization,* Celestial Arts (1973), revised edition, Blackwell (1990).
3. Taylor, F. W., *Principles of Scientific Management,* Harper (1911).
4. Weber, M., *The Theory of Social and Economic Organization,* Free Press (1943).
5. Koontz, H. and C. O'Donnell, *The Principles of Management,* McGraw-Hill (1968).
6. Drucker, P., *Management: Tasks, Responsibilities and Practices,* Pan (1979).
7. Peters, T. and B. Waterman, *In Search of Excellence,* Harper & Row (1982).
8. Handy, C., *The Age of Unreason,* Business Books (1989).
9. Deming, W. E., *Out of the Crisis,* Cambridge University Press (1988).

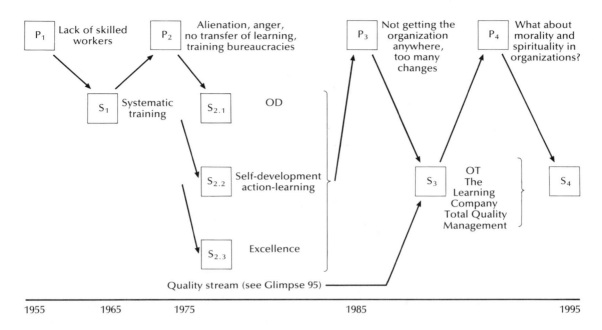

Figure 2.9 From systematic training to the Learning Company

10.   Owen, H., *Spirit: Transformation and Development in Organizations*, Abbott Publishing (1987).
11.   Boydell, T. H., *A Guide to Job Analysis*, Bacie (1970).
12.   Boydell, T. H. and M. J. Pedler, (eds), *Management Self-Development: Concepts and Practices*, Gower (1981).

3. Are you a Learning Company?

In Chapter 1 we looked at the evolution of the idea of the Learning Company and saw that it flows from various streams of thought – about learning, organizations, training and development and management of quality. Now we can look in a certain amount of detail at the Learning Company itself. What is it? How would we recognize it? How does it differ from a *non*-Learning Company?

In trying to answer these questions we have used three sets of sources; our speculative ideas about what the Learning Company ought to be, based on the apparent next steps in the evolutionary flow; the ideas of other workers in this field, including Argyris and Schon,[1] Revans,[2] Deming[3] and our research in a number of companies, as reported in detail in Pedler, Boydell and Burgoyne[4] with subsequent modifications in the light of more recent data.

From the latter came a list of 11 dimensions or features of a Learning Company.

The characteristics of a Learning Company

The learning approach to strategy

By this we mean that company policy and strategy formation, together with implementation, evaluation and improvement, are consciously structured as a learning process. In that sense it is not a gung-ho approach, but one that allows business plans to be developed, formulated and revised as you go along. Managerial acts are thus seen as conscious experiments, rather than set solutions. Deliberate small-scale experiments and feedback loops are built into the planning process to enable continuous improvement in the light of experience. (Interestingly, the words 'experiment' and 'experience' come from the same root.) For example, the decision by Pilkington's about where to build their new glass plant (see Glimpse 57) shows how flexible strategy-making policies can allow decisions to emerge in the face of conflicting pressures.

Participative policy-making

This characteristic refers to the sharing of involvement in the policy- and strategy-forming processes. That is, all members of the company have a chance to take part, to discuss and contribute to major policy decisions. There is a deliberate fostering and encouragement of contributions and a recognition that successful debate involves working *with* tensions, or even conflicts, between different values, positions and views. There is a commitment to airing differences and working through conflicts as the way to reaching business decisions that all members are likely to support.

Who are these 'members' of the company? The legal definition is, in effect, restricted to the owners, but the Learning Company takes a much broader view and thus 'members' will come from a wide range of stakeholders. These include different groupings of employees, customers, suppliers, owners and neighbours, including the community and the environment. Within these groupings there will be significant sub-sets of diversity, such as women, men, black, white, different nationalities or geographic origins, young, old, differing degrees of physical or mental ability, different learning styles and needs, different political or spiritual beliefs, different levels of formal education, different social classes (certainly in the UK, and probably in most societies), different personal styles, temperaments, inner qualities, modes of managing and so on.

Participative policy making requires three fundamental attitudes towards this diversity, namely:

- that all diverse groups have the *right* to take part, for their values and so on to be taken into account – this is the *ethical* or *moral* dimension of the Learning Company
- that such diversity, although complicated, is, in fact, valuable in that it leads to creativity, to better ideas and solutions
- that only by striving to delight customers and meet the requirements of other stakeholders will the company be successful in the long-term achievement of its purpose (we use the word 'delight' here to indicate that just *matching* customer requirements or *satisfying* them is not enough as customers like to be pleased and sometimes surprised by the quality of service and so delighting them includes looking over the horizon, doing something that at present the customers are not aware that they want – nobody asked for an electric light bulb, but somebody provided one).

To work effectively with such diversity requires high levels of self-awareness and a thorough understanding of ways of handling and redeeming conflict. Companies may need to develop special procedures to legitimate and harness this diversity and richness. The hotel group, which used the search conferencing approach (see Glimpse 16) and the method of learning from dialectic (see Glimpse 6), shows examples of this.

Finally, what is the role of competitors in the Learning Company? Are they stakeholders? This is such an important issue that we examine it specifically under the heading 'Boundary workers as environmental scanners' below.

Informating

This describes the state of affairs in which information technology is used to inform and empower people rather than, as so often is the case at present, disempower them. This involves three major shifts in attitude or perspective about:

- to whom information is made available, that is, make it widely available as possible
- the use to which it is put – not to reward (and hence punish) or have control over or report on or keep in storage just in case, but, rather, understand what is happening in the company's systems and processes
- understanding the nature of data, in particular, that *all* systems and processes have some natural or inherent variation in their output, therefore, when interpreting data it is essential to find out if:
  - it is just representative of the inherent variation – if so, the system is said to be 'in control' and the only way to improve the output is by carefully and scientifically working on the system
  - something unusual is happening in the system, such that the output cannot be explained by the inherent variation – in this case, the system is said to be 'out of control' and, before we can say or do anything about its capability, we must investigate these special causes of abnormal variation.

At the same time, of course, we need specific information systems (which must themselves be *in control*!) to make data available. Thus, information technology and public domain databases empower others who can 'interrogate' or 'dialogue' with them, in ways that are empowering, interesting, fun to use and lead to learning.

Formative accounting and control

This is in part a particular case or application of informating. We have given it a separate specific characteristic because of the key importance given to accounting and budgeting systems in most companies.

Formative accounting, then, ensures that systems of accounting, budgeting and reporting are structured to assist learning, and hence delight their internal customers. This is the way in which such systems add value to the company. In fact, although this sounds simple, it represents a huge change in perspective. Asking those who run a control system who their customers are and what would delight them is a radical shift.

At the same time, there is an ethos of self-responsibility, with the development of systems that encourage individuals and units to act as small businesses within a regulated environment. Again, as with informating in general, the emphasis is upon auditing, managing and accounting for actions.

Internal exchange involves all internal units and departments seeing themselves as customers and suppliers, contracting with one another in a partly regulated market economy. The purpose of a department is thus to 'delight' its internal customer. To do so, individuals, groups, departments and divisions engage in constant dialogue – exchanging information on expectations, negotiating, contracting and giving feedback on goods or services received. Since our purpose is to delight our internal customer, the latter is seen as the key stakeholder. At the same time, internal customers recognize that their suppliers have rights and needs too, and treat them with respect. In any case, it is fully understood that the way to deliver quality is to receive it – hence we need good relationships with our suppliers in order to develop good relationships with our customers.

Another key element here is that of overall collaboration, rather than competition. Thus, each department not only seeks to delight its customer, and vice versa (mutual win:win), but, also, everybody remains aware of the needs of the company as a whole. This calls for further levels of discussion, negotiation and contracting in a spirit of *overall* win:win, to ensure that certain units are not delighting *their* internal customers in such a way as to prevent others from doing the same. By this collaboration there is an overall optimization of performance.

In tune with ideas about increasing degrees of participation, we also need to start to explore new, alternative ways of rewarding people in a Learning Company.

First, we need to recognize that money need not be the sole reward and that for many people a whole range of things might be considered 'rewarding' (see Glimpse 100). However, when it comes to financial reward, perhaps we need to question some of the assumptions we make about payments. *Why* do we pay some people more than others? *What* values or assumptions are we making about the basis of pay? Why do we *pay* people at all? To satisfy their needs as human beings? To encourage them to work harder? To persuade them to work for us rather than for another competitor? To buy their skills? To prevent them from withholding their skills from us? To ensure that they vote for us at the next election (of directors or of government)? To satisfy a need for justice and fair shares?

Each one of the answers to these questions seems to have formed the basis for various systems and processes for working out wage and salary levels. To the extent that participants in any given process are in agreement with the underlying principle, they will be happy with that process. Often, though, the underlying assumptions are unstated, hidden, unrecognized. In a Learning Company these will be brought out into the open, shared, examined and alternatives will be discussed and tried out.

This is probably the most difficult of the 11 characteristics on which to make progress, since it is likely to involve changing not only the distribution of reward, but also the distribution of power. Several of the other characteristics imply this redistribution of power from the 'top pyramid' to the wider company.

Enabling structures

Such structures create opportunities for individual and business development. Roles are loosely structured, in line with the established and contracted needs of internal customers and suppliers, and in such a way as to allow for personal growth and experiment. Thus, departmental and other boundaries are seen as temporary structures that can flex in response to changes. The aim is to create an organizational architecture that gives space and headroom for meeting current needs and responding to future changes.

New *forms* of structure will be needed. We have seen in Chapter 1 how pictures of structures have evolved; we now need to know how pictures of structures have evolved; we now need to experiment with new ones.

Boundary workers as environmental scanners

Just as informating takes place within the company, so is data collected from outside. Although there may be people or departments who specialize in this, in a Learning Company such scanning is carried out by *all* members who have contact with external customers, clients, suppliers, neighbours and so on. These boundary workers deliver goods and services, receive supplies and orders *and* systematically collect and carry back information that is collated and disseminated. For example, at Rank-Xerox, sales people are seen as information *gatherers* just as much as product *sellers*. At Radio Rentals, technicians who go out to repair or adjust equipment are being seen more and more as sources of information on what customers want next.

Inter-company learning

Since a Learning Company seeks to delight its customers, it will engage in a number of mutually advantageous learning activities. Joint training, sharing in investment, in research and development, job exchanges – these are just some of the ways in which this takes place. The corollary, of course, is that it also joins with its suppliers in these activities. We can also learn from companies in other industries

– a process often known as 'benchmarking'. For example, Rank-Xerox set out to learn from Caterpillar, considered to be the world's best company (i.e., the benchmark) at delivering heavy equipment.

More surprisingly, perhaps, competitors get together for mutual learning. They don't fight each other (win:lose, which in the long run always leads to sub-optimization, or, lose:lose), but engage in win:win learning. They recognize that both their interests will be served by increasing the market, bringing in technological advances, establishing joint industry standards, and so on. Rank-Xerox have a slogan 'come and steal shamelessly from us'.

Learning climate

In a Learning Company managers see their primary task as facilitating members' experimentation and learning from experience. It is normal to take time out to seek feedback, to obtain data to aid understanding. Senior managers give a lead in questioning their own ideas, attitudes and actions. Mistakes are allowed – if not exactly encouraged – for it is recognized that we will never learn if we don't try out new ideas, new ways of doing things, and these won't always work. We need to recognize that there's no such thing as a failed experiment – as long as we learn from it. External stakeholders – customers, suppliers, owners, neighbours, competitors – are all involved in these processes. Similarly, there is a strong realization that differences, as discussed under 'Participative policy making' earlier, are essential for learning.

Importance is attached to the idea of continuous improvement. We can *always* learn and do better, no matter how well we think we are doing at present: 'good enough is not good enough', we always need to be striving to do even better.

Self-development opportunities for all

Resources and facilities for self-development are made available to all members of the company – employees at all levels, and, ideally, external stakeholders, too. With appropriate guidance, including systems for feeding back data, people are encouraged to take responsibility for their own learning and development.

A whole range of resources will be required. These will include courses, workshops, seminars, self-learning materials, but in addition there will be others, such as development groups, one-to-one coaching/mentoring, peer-level one-to-one co-counselling. Databanks will provide information on what is available, together with, on a voluntary opting-in basis, details of individuals who are working on specific developmental issues and who are looking, got or are willing to give support and mutual guidance.

Learning Company profile

These, then, are the 11 characteristics of the Learning Company as we see them. In the remainder of this chapter we will take a further look at these, and develop a more general model of the Learning Company, drawing out some of the underlying principles that seem to be emerging

At this point, however, you may wish to think about your own company and to what extent it matches these characteristics.

To do a proper diagnosis you would need to survey across the whole of the company – including external stakeholders. If you wish to do that, an instrument is available from us at the Learning Company Project (the address is given on page 213). On a smaller, less formal scale, however, you might like to use the Learning Company profile of Figure 3.1, (pages 26–27). This is designed to give an overview of each of the 11 characteristics. You and your colleagues, perhaps after discussion together, can then give a score for your company on each characteristic, entering it in the square box in each of the 11 areas (it can be on a scale of 1 to 10, 1 to 5 or whatever you choose.)

Modelling the Learning Company

As noted above, the 11 characteristics of the Learning Company described in the first part of this chapter, emerged from our early research. At this point they were a list of features referred to in the literature and by managers in companies. There was no necessary relationship between one characteristic and another, although it seemed probable that various linkages were likely to exist. Is there enough of a relationship between these 11 characteristics or features to justify our suggestion that here is a model (that is, a *simplified* representation indicating how the various parts of the company interact and fit together) of the Learning Company?

Since compiling the original list we have spent a lot of time seeking this ideal. The list, in effect, was what we might call the primal forum for a possible model – each part being concrete and actual but with no indication of how these parts formed the whole. In its original form there was no particular order or sequence to the 11 points. We have presented them here in a particular order, based on the model described in the next few pages.

The first step in our modelling process was to attempt to order and cluster the 11 characteristics.

The 'blueprint'

Our original list, you will recall, had no order to it, but further examination sug-gested that it could be presented in a semi-diagrammatic form, as in Figure 3.2, where each of the 11 points have 5 clusters that are aspects of those points. The central pivot, as it were, is Structures. Above this we have Looking in and below it Looking out, the mirror-image of Looking in. Above Looking in, we have Strategy and at the bottom, Learning opportunities, the mirror of Strategy.

For certain purposes this second-generation picture is preferable to the preceding descriptions. It provides a neat, one-page summary, eminently suited for presentations, and it does show the relationships between the clusters, as we have seen.

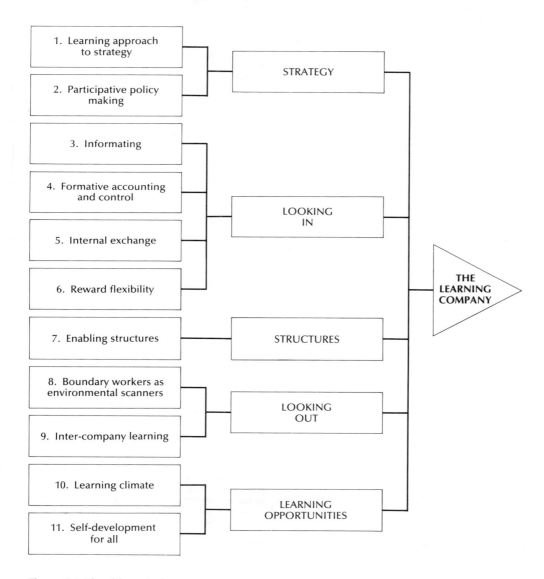

Figure 3.2 The 'blueprint'

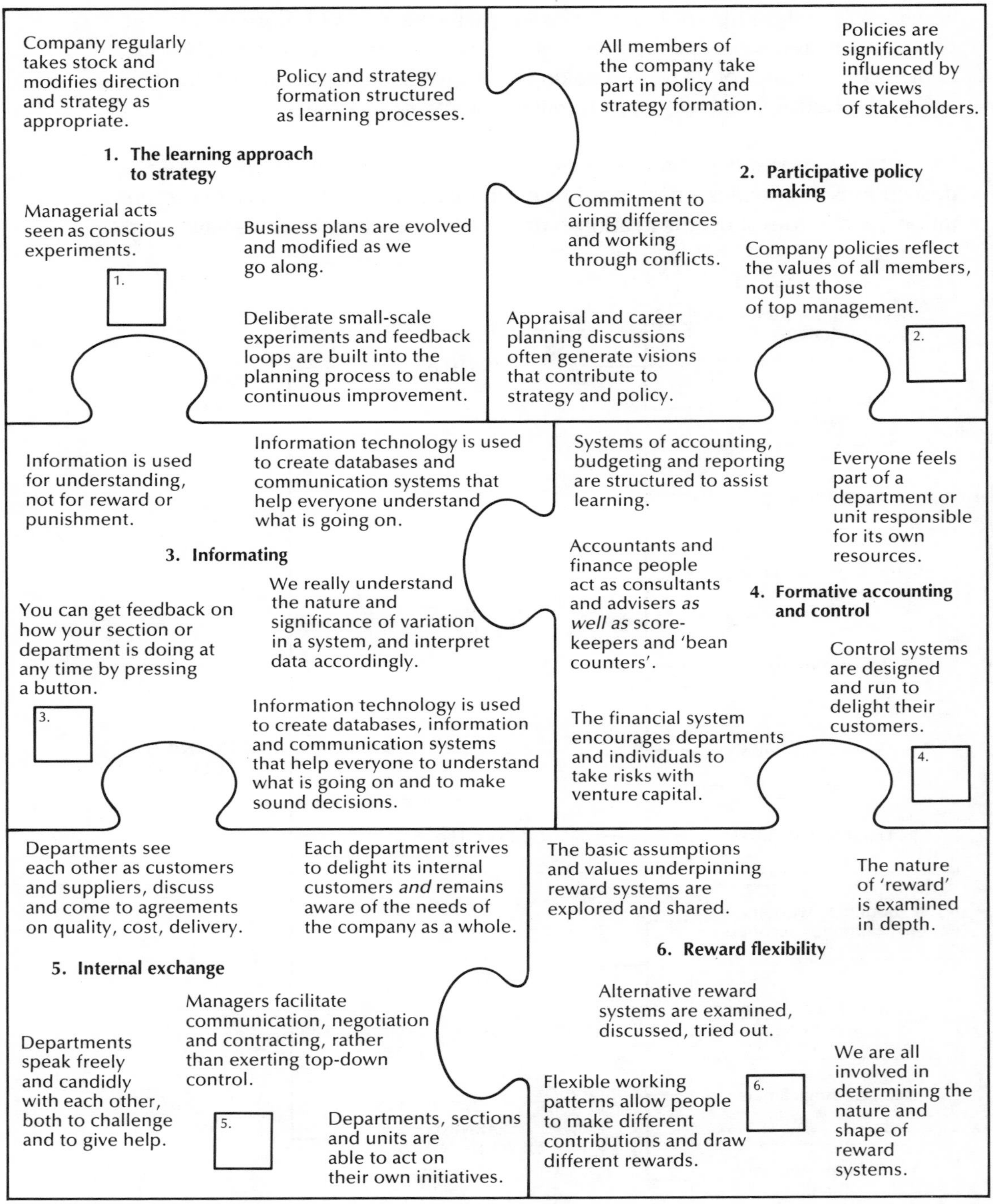

Company regularly takes stock and modifies direction and strategy as appropriate.

Policy and strategy formation structured as learning processes.

All members of the company take part in policy and strategy formation.

Policies are significantly influenced by the views of stakeholders.

1. The learning approach to strategy

Managerial acts seen as conscious experiments.

1.

Business plans are evolved and modified as we go along.

Deliberate small-scale experiments and feedback loops are built into the planning process to enable continuous improvement.

Commitment to airing differences and working through conflicts.

Appraisal and career planning discussions often generate visions that contribute to strategy and policy.

2. Participative policy making

Company policies reflect the values of all members, not just those of top management.

2.

Information is used for understanding, not for reward or punishment.

Information technology is used to create databases and communication systems that help everyone understand what is going on.

Systems of accounting, budgeting and reporting are structured to assist learning.

Everyone feels part of a department or unit responsible for its own resources.

3. Informating

You can get feedback on how your section or department is doing at any time by pressing a button.

3.

We really understand the nature and significance of variation in a system, and interpret data accordingly.

Information technology is used to create databases, information and communication systems that help everyone to understand what is going on and to make sound decisions.

Accountants and finance people act as consultants and advisers *as well as* score-keepers and 'bean counters'.

The financial system encourages departments and individuals to take risks with venture capital.

4. Formative accounting and control

Control systems are designed and run to delight their customers.

4.

Departments see each other as customers and suppliers, discuss and come to agreements on quality, cost, delivery.

Each department strives to delight its internal customers *and* remains aware of the needs of the company as a whole.

The basic assumptions and values underpinning reward systems are explored and shared.

The nature of 'reward' is examined in depth.

5. Internal exchange

Departments speak freely and candidly with each other, both to challenge and to give help.

Managers facilitate communication, negotiation and contracting, rather than exerting top-down control.

5.

Departments, sections and units are able to act on their own initiatives.

6. Reward flexibility

Alternative reward systems are examined, discussed, tried out.

Flexible working patterns allow people to make different contributions and draw different rewards.

6.

We are all involved in determining the nature and shape of reward systems.

Figure 3.1 Learning Company profile

Roles and careers are flexibly structured to allow for experimentation, growth and adaptation.

Appraisals are geared more to learning and development than to reward and punishment.

It is part of the work of all staff to collect, bring back, and report information about what's going on outside the company.

All meetings in the company regularly include a review of what's going on in our business environment.

8. Boundary workers as environmental scanners

7. Enabling structures

Departmental and other boundaries are seen as temporary structures that can flex in response to changes.

We have rules and procedures but they are frequently changed after review and discussion.

7.

We meet regularly with representative groups of customers, suppliers, community members and so on to find out what's important to them.

We receive regular intelligence reports on the economy, markets, technological developments, socio-political events and world trends and examine how these may affect our business.

We experiment with new forms of structures.

There are systems and procedures for receiving, collating and sharing information from outside the company.

8.

People from the company go on attachments to our business partners, including suppliers, customers and competitors.

If something goes wrong around here you can expect help, support, and interest in learning lessons from it.

People make time to question their own practice, to analyse, discuss and learn from what happens.

We regularly meet with our competitors to share ideas and information.

9. Inter-company learning

10. Learning climate

We participate in joint learning events with our suppliers, customers and other stakeholders.

9.

There is a general attitude of continuous improvement — always trying to learn and do better.

10.

When you don't know something, it's normal to ask around until you get the required help or information.

We engage in joint ventures with our suppliers, customers and competitors, to develop new products and markets.

We use benchmarking in order to learn from the best practice in other industries.

Differences of all sorts, between young and old, women and men, black and white, etc. are recognized and positively valued as essential to learning and creativity.

People here have their own self-development budgets — they decide what training and development they want, and what to pay for it.

11. Self-development opportunities for all

There are lots of opportunities, materials and resources available for learning on an 'open access' basis around the company.

11.

Self-development resources are available to external stakeholders.

The exploration of an individual's learning needs is the central focus of appraisal and career planning.

With appropriate guidance people are encouraged to take responsibility.

Figure 3.1 cont'd

On the other hand, this representation is somewhat rigid. It is mechanical, fixed, static. It implies completeness with no room for extra characteristics, as yet unrecognized. For us, too, it has rather too little aesthetic appeal. We might call this stage the rational/mechanical, implying that this is a blueprint as yet lacking life.

The 'fountain tree' picture

We therefore began to experiment with alternative forms. The first was the straightforward fishbone diagram you see in Figure 3.3.

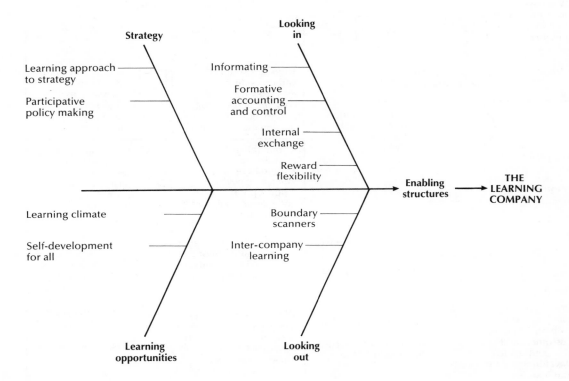

Figure 3.3 The fishbone

This has a certain appeal – it is firm, clear, rational concise – but it is still static.

Turning the fishbone through 90° produced a fir tree model (Figure 3.4), which got us experimenting with trees as a form. The final outcome of this line of thought was a combination of a tree and a fountain – the 'fountain tree' of Figure 3.5.

This too has strengths and weaknesses as a model. It is less clear and concise than the fishbone, but perhaps that is a strength? After all, the notion of a Learning

Figure 3.4 The fir tree

Company is far from clear and concise – it is living, evolving, changing – hence we have deliberately left some branches/sprays of the fountain tree unlabelled.

Again, the fountain tree is full of energy. Water, or sap, or life forces, flow up the middle, outwards, downwards, and then into the middle again. There is an element of dynamic ecological balance here that somehow seems characteristic of a Learning Company. It is the people who provide the energy that needs to rise up the company (as modern Human Resource management ideas recognize). People give their energies to the collective purpose of the company and that creates the shared identity that is not a fixed, once-and-forever phenomenon, but a continuously produced quality of people's interactions.

The fountain tree represents the *organic* or *living* phase of our modelling process.

The Learning Company as energy flow: the symbolic stage

It was this element of *flow* that inspired us to represent our ideas in another way. This time the flow is of energy and the picture is more abstract. The 11 characteristics of a Learning Company no longer feature explicitly and our model has become more symbolic and mysterious, less concrete and more abstract.

In the energy flow model, Figure 3.6, there are four double loops or figure eights. The first two of these are horizontal and represent the energy flow of the person between ideas and action, and vice versa, and the collective energy flow of the company between policy and operations, and vice versa. The 'policy' and 'ideas' loops are mainly concerned with 'inner' activities, while the 'operation' and 'action' loops are more concerned with outer affairs.

This pair of double loops is strongly related to Characteristic 1, the Learning approach to strategy, and 10, the Learning climate, in that feedback from action and operations is the source of our individual and collective learning and the creativity of our ideas and policies enrich the productivity of our outputs.

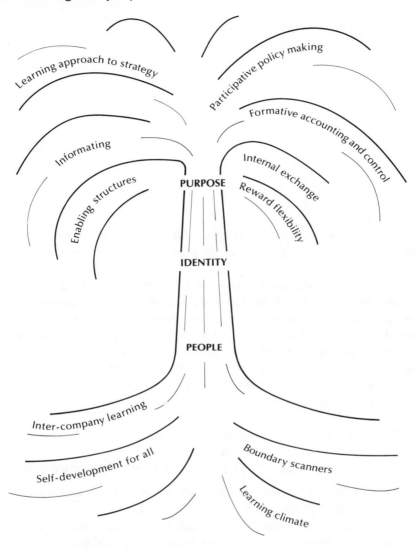

Figure 3.5 The fountain tree

However, for the Learning Company to come to life, there must also be constant energy flows and connections between the individual and collective levels. This gives us the second vertical pair of double loops you can see in Figure 3.7.

This third double loop is clearly related to our first two characteristics, the Learning approach to strategy and participative policy making.

The fourth double loop shows how the energy of individual action must connect

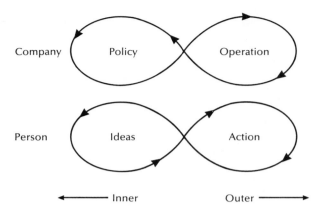

Figure 3.6 Energy flow in the symbolic stage

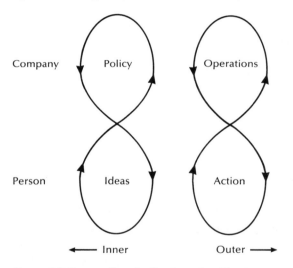

Figure 3.7 Energy flow in the Learning Company

with and infuse the collective operation. In return, the way we work together feeds individual motivation and the propensity to act.

Putting the four figures of eight together we create an energy flow model (see Figure 3.8) with a number of interesting aspects:

First, a vertical energy flow links and mutually enriches collective purpose with individual purposes; collective identity with personal identity. Individual purpose comes about through shared identity, which, in turn, fires our collective purpose. Equally, collective purpose gives meaning to our lives and our place in the company.

Second, horizontal energy flows link vision with action. Inner searching, which leads to company policy, is realized through collective operations and individual

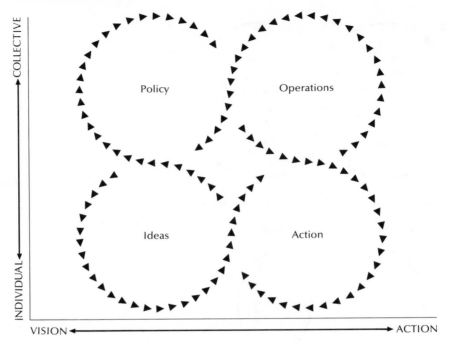

Figure 3.8 The energy flow model

actions realize the learning and development of the people in the company. We never stop learning and developing and, in that sense, we are all of us searching for the next expression and realization of our identities. This is one of the major functions of management and people-development activities and of the overall learning climate of the company. Just as individuals seek to extend themselves, so the company as a whole, in its learning approach to strategy, seeks to find the next expression of collective identity and purpose – what are *we* here for now? The Learning Company does not arrive except temporarily.

Third, there are many elaborations and ways in which the energy flow model can be used, most of which require considerable further research and development work. For example:

- where does energy start to flow and where is the best place to make a start?
- can energy flow directly from the operations into the ideas lobe or from the policy into the action lobe or must it go through the connecting lobe?
- what happens when you get stuck in one lobe? There are many companies that are unbalanced in their development – all operations with little policy develop-ment or full of individual action but with little in the way of new ideas and learning; equally there are those companies that spend a great deal of time searching and somehow do not realize their full potential

- what is the significance of the cross-over points or slips? (there are two of these on each double loop – eight in all – each having different characteristics – for example, the feedback from operations into policy is different from the linkage between individual actions and collective operations, but they also have some connection – and slips, which should be open in the Learning Company to allow full and free energy flow, will often be stuck or blocked in practice and opening up the slips between the lobes will require careful diagnosis and specific intervention).

These and many other possibilities for diagnosis and action are opened up by the energy flow model. It needs further work, and this we are now doing.

Conclusion

This chapter forms the core of this book in that it presents the main dimensions of the Learning Company idea as we see them. It also offers you a means of making a start in your own company.

The work is necessarily incomplete. We have included all our thinking about the Learning Company model because we feel that all the different pictures have merit. You may prefer earlier ones to later ones, you may be able to develop better ones – we hope so. All we would ask in return is that you send us a copy and we will be glad to share further thoughts with you.

REFERENCES

1. Argyris, C. and D. A. Schon, *Organizational Learning: A Theory in Action Perspective*, Addison-Wesley (1978).
2. Revans, R. W., 'The Enterprise as a Learning System' in R. W. Revans *The Origins and Growth of Action Learning*, Chartwell-Bratt (1982).
3. Deming, W. E., *Out of the Crisis*, Cambridge University Press (1988).
4. Pedler, M. J., T. H. Boydell and J. G. Burgoyne, *Learning Company Project Report*, Manpower Services Commission (May 1988).

4. The biography of your company

Seen as organisms, companies are dynamic. Every year many thousands are brought to life by hopeful people and every year many also die through bankruptcy, takeover or simply ceasing trading. Infant mortality of companies is very high – 40 or 50 per cent is not unusual in the first year. Once established, companies do not stay the same for very long (although it may sometimes appear so from the inside). They pass through a number of life stages from birth to maturity and, just as human beings encounter problems as they pass from childhood to adolescence to adulthood, these passages in the life of a company can be stormy, marked by crisis and turbulence.

Companies differ from people in one respect. There is no more or less fixed life span. We have companies that are 200 years old and, as far as we know, no individual human being can manage this. However, the life cycle image holds up reasonably well. Companies *do* experience birth, death and the stages in between. There is an obvious link between the death of large 'household name' manufacturing concerns, on which we have come to rely for jobs and wealth, and the new small businesses that are springing up in their wake.

Companies, like people, are unique in their purposes and identity. Each one faces particular problems and circumstances. At the same time there are questions that are predictable at different stages of the company life cycle – just as young adults, newly independent, typically experience similar problems. So, for example, the young company, full of the drive and vision of its founders, will struggle and perhaps not survive the crisis caused when the founders later leave or retire. If it does survive, the company will do so because it finds a new way of doing things. This new way will work well, that is until new problems emerge that demand attention. This is the cycle of development. Our actions, which resolve the old problems, also create the conditions in which the new ones will eventually arise. There is no cheating this law, for this is the story of developing – taking our next step, dealing with the 'now' problems, within the context of the life cycle.

The Learning Company is marked by an acceptance of this law and an awareness that things do not stay the same for long. In the Learning Company we know that developing from one stage to another is not easy, that crisis and conflict cannot be avoided in the move from the old to the new. Like other companies, the Learning Company does not know what its future is, but it does have a picture of what it *wants* it to be. Moreover, it has developed the capacity among all its members to contribute to this picture and an understanding by them of the processes of development – of *how* you get there.

This chapter aims to help you to develop a biography of your company. It contains some ideas and suggestions for getting a picture of the *past* – where you have been and what has made you the company you are today – the *present* – where you are now and what issues and questions are coming your way – and *the future* – where you are going and what your first steps might be. This chapter takes the form of an activity for members, working in a representative group, to construct a biography of the company. While this activity can be done in a single session, there is much to be said for working on it over a longer period of time. This basic process can be much elaborated.

Company biography activity

Step 1

First you need a group of people. This could be the whole company, if it is quite small, it could be the board of directors, although this is not very representative, it could be a group representing all the main parts of the company – as in the Search conference design (see Glimpse 16) or it could be any interested group of people.

Chapter 5, which discusses various starting points for the Learning Company project, may be helpful at this stage. Spending time here thinking through who should be in this group, how it is set up, how people are invited and so on and the implications of creating a shared story together is well worth while.

Step 2

Give each person a blank copy of the lifeline graph (Figure 4.1) and ask each person to consider where they think the company is now. Put a master chart on the wall and ask each person to put a cross on the line that expresses their view.

What is the overall picture? Is there a consensus or a wide variation? Discuss your collective plot of crosses before moving on.

Step 3

As a check on your own interpretation of where the company is now, here is a set of questions attached to each of the seven stages of the company given in Figure

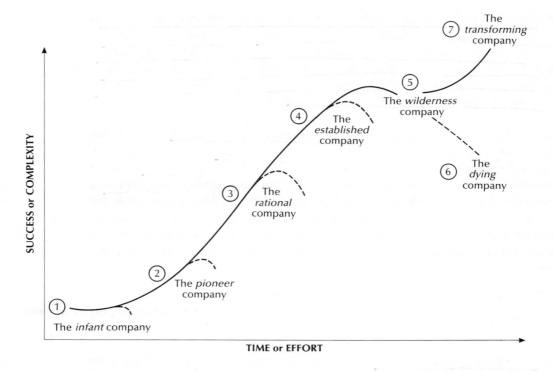

Figure 4.1 The life stages of a company

4.1.* Break into small groups to discuss these questions and find out if the answers confirm your intuitive positioning of your company.

1. The *infant* company is a brand new start-up by an individual entrepreneur or group or it can be a new project, department or section in an existing company, or a joint venture between existing companies.

Key questions at this stage are:

• what is our vision of the company?
• what does the company exist for; what is its purpose?
• what does the company look like and feel like?
• how can the vision be turned into reality?

---

* Though presented in a linear progression here, companies may skip stages or visit them in a different sequence. For example, a company can be faced with the dying or transforming stages at almost any point. It is worth stressing here that the idea of the Learning Company is not the corporate answer to immortality – companies *should* die to make room for new life when their purpose has been accomplished. The Learning Company is one that recognizes this and works always with a sense of its own mortality and life span.

- what resources – people, money, equipment, etc., are needed?
- what are our products and how are they marketed?

2. The *pioneer* company is small and fast-growing with a central, powerful figure or group driving it.

Key questions at this stage are:

- do we stay small or get bigger?
- if we grow, what new systems do we need to cope with expansion?
- what new people do we need and how will they be integrated?
- who can replace the leader(s) and what plans do we have for succession?
- do we need a new leadership style?

3. The *rational* company has outgrown its initiators and become independent, bigger and more complex.

Key questions at this stage are:

- are the founders really in touch with the business needs now?
- is the management style too authoritarian, too personal?
- how can we use systems to bring order, rationality, consistency and fairness?
- what new procedures are needed to manage our people?
- what specialist functions do we need, e.g., sales, personnel, R & D?

4. The *established* company is just that – well set up with formal procedures and scientific management applied to most aspects of its functioning.

Key questions at this stage are:

- how can we encourage entrepreneurship, risk-taking and motivation?
- how can we minimize red tape, rigidity and bureaucracy?
- what can be done about the barriers between departments and functions?
- can we decentralize and give more autonomy to front-line departments?
- are we getting bored with our business?

5. The *wilderness* company has lost its way and got out of touch.

Key questions at this stage are:

- how can we change our relationship with our customers and suppliers?
- do we have the right clients?
- how can we change our view of the outside world from one that is full of enemies and threats to one which is full of opportunities and potential allies?
- what are we here for?
- what should our new purpose be?

6. The *dying* company is one that is failing or bankrupt or where the purpose of its being has been completed.

Key questions at this stage are:

- is it time for the company to die?
- should we make a good end or try to create new life through merger, 'surgery', management buyout, etc.?
- what are our moral obligations to stakeholders – shareholders, employees, customers, suppliers and the community?
- what new seeds can spring from the husk of the company?

7. The *transforming* company is one that has decided that now is not the time to die and has found new purpose, new identity, new life.

Key questions at this stage are similar to those for the infant company, except that they have a conscious awareness of the past:

- what is our new vision and what is our purpose for being in business now?
- who are our new customers and what new services are we offering our old ones?
- how are we going to work differently to accomplish our vision and goals?
- how can we learn from what we are doing?
- how do we organize ourselves for learning?

Step 4

Having established some consensus on the question of where you are on the lifeline, now it is time to focus on the past and consider some of the events and decisions that have made the company what it is today. To do this, ask each person or small group, to list the *key* company development events of the last years. The number of years you go back depends on several things. It isn't a problem for newish companies, but for an older one, you have to balance the weight of history with the need for focusing on the present. You could focus on the last 3, 5 or 10 years or you could allow people to go back further and perhaps ration the number of events to 12 or 20.

When people have had time to decide on their events, have them plot these on a time chart similar to Figure 4.1, but this time showing history to the present. You can have peaks and troughs to indicate the type of event. Figure 4.2 shows a made up example.

Whether you have people or groups presenting different interpretations of key events or whether you just have one master chart and try to get consensus around important turning points, it is important to notice

- what is *agreed*
- what is *not* agreed.

Some events will be remembered and construed in a similar fashion by members,

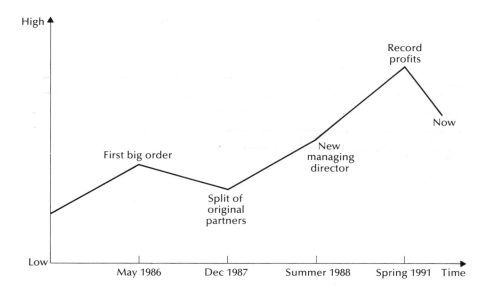

Figure 4.2 Key company development events

but where there are significant events on some lists and not on others or where the same event is remembered very differently, then these may contain critical clues to the identity of the company. Why is there a different memory? What is the effect of this upon current operations? What could be done to honour or redeem this past event.

Warning – this kind of delving into history is not for the weak-kneed. Under despots, historians often become dissidents. Going through the company's history together will turn over stones and who is to say what skeletons may be discovered. However, it is also through patient archaeology that we discover our origins and identity. When we are seeking a shared purpose and future this can be a powerful and essential first step.

Now, looking at the gaps or spaces between events, what phases or periods are described here? Could you put names to them? You can use song or book titles to do this – 'Singing the Blues' or 'A Tale of Two Cities' and so on. You may find that these phases link up with some of those in Figure 4.1.

When you have a sense of the phases the company has been through, look for the themes or threads that run through the company's life so far. Themes are harder to detect than events or phases, sometimes muted by the more dramatic happenings, sometimes intermittent, here now, gone there and reappearing again. There could be a theme concerning the type of conflicts experienced within the company, of inventiveness, of public spiritedness, of short-termism, of insecurity, of an insistence on high quality.

List as many themes as people can spot. Themes are particularly important to spot because they tend to live on and affect things at a deep level though not necessarily in a dramatic way. While history is unlikely to repeat itself with regard to actual events or phases, it is the *themes* that come back either to support or to haunt us and which give us this sense of *déjà vu*.

Now work through the following questions in the whole group or in small groups:

- which of these themes live on in the present?
- which of them are positive ones to build on?
- which themes are negative ones that should be finally laid to rest or redeemed in some way?
- which themes have disappeared that we could bring back in a positive way?

As a result of this theme-work, do you have some indicators of what the future may bring or perhaps how we might react to what the future may bring?

Step 5

You may be relieved to know that at this point we are back in the present. Before we go on, there is a method underlying the activities in this company biography activity. This is know as the 'U curve', and like many of our ideas about how to do biography, it comes to us from the NPI Consulting Group in the Netherlands (see Figure 4.3).

As you can see, we have been following the U curve since the beginning of Step 4, tracing a route through the past to read, interpret and re-interpret company history as a preparation for diagnosis of our present state and future intentions.

One way of diagnosing your present state is to use the Learning Company profile (LCP) on pages 26–27. Although we deal with past, present and future in this company biography activity, we deal with the same progression on a broader scale in this book as a whole. Thus, this chapter being about biography is mainly past-oriented, as you'd expect, while Chapter 3, which contains the LCP, is essentially centred on the now, the present. The earlier and later parts of the book are focused on the future – to offer a vision of the Learning Company and some ideas or 'Glimpses' of how it may be achieved.

Apart from the LCP, there are many other ways to work on the present. This step is about taking stock of the current situation – what are our strengths, our weaknesses? What opportunities and threats are there for us now? Another way is to map out your stakeholders:

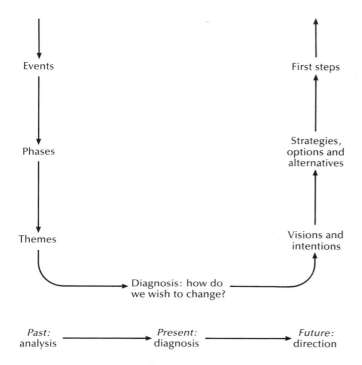

Figure 4.3 The U curve of company biography

- your customers
- your suppliers
- your trading and venture partners
- your local communities
- and the wider world.

Ask yourselves – individually, in small groups and together – what questions are each of these groups putting to us? Go through all your stakeholders in turn. Before moving on, ask yourselves what questions are we posing for ourselves? Not only, what is it that we want, but also what are we puzzled, concerned, interested or intrigued by?

It is important to take time to consider each question and each stakeholder in turn, because we are so adept at tuning out awkward and inconvenient questions. If you wish to be really adventurous, why not invite some representatives of these stakeholder groups to join in at this point in the company biography activity?

Before you leave the present, you should be able to formulate some of the key questions that will guide the company's future. What are these questions? Are they 'Why?' questions, needing further research, or are they of the 'How can we . . . ?' variety that lead on to vision and strategy? The fundamental questions underlying the diagnosis of your present are, 'Do we wish to change?' and 'Why?'

Step 6

When we move down the left-hand side of the U curve, our analysis becomes deeper as we look for fundamental characteristics and themes. As we come out of the present and move into the future-focused right-hand side, we reverse this movement, starting with abstract ideas and visions and ending with concrete first steps.

Let's look at your visions and intentions, assuming that your diagnostic work up to and including Step 5 has led you to a desire for change and has focused the necessary dissatisfaction with aspects of the present state of the company. Now we need to work imaginatively to construct some ideas and visions about where we want to go next. It can help at this stage to use artistic and non-verbal methods such as painting, clay modelling, group sculpting, music or dance to free up the vision. Unless you are very unusual, there will be someone in your group who has some skills and experience to offer here.

This is a point of some importance. If you do wish to employ imaginative, artistic ideas, you may think first of asking for outside help. This *may* be a good thing, but it *can* result in not building upon and realizing your own resources. If you do use an external person – at this point, or at any other – always ensure that you have a strategy for learning the skill or quality that that person brings. The Learning Company welcomes many visitors and part of the contract is that they come to learn *and* to teach.

There are various activities in this book that will help you construct ideas and visions, for example, see Glimpses 5 and 42.

Once you have some idea of where you want to go – some concepts, ideas, visions and intentions that you want to realize – the next step is to create some alternatives and options. Differences and debate are important here in order to provide options and to test your chosen directions. Glimpses 6 and 40 may help here in terms of encouraging people to generate and debate some alternatives.

Likely scenarios can be constructed and tried out on the wider company members who can be asked to comment on and offer amendments to these alternative visions of the future. In terms of consulting with everyone on the future direction and identity of the company, the 'architectural competition' is a way of proceeding. Have the proponents of the various ideas present them in some form, perhaps in a special newsletter with a voting form attached for readers, then announce the results, give prizes and explain the final choice.

First steps can be reached via the Strategic Staircase (see Glimpse 75). Working backwards from your chosen vision, what do we need to do by when to get from now to then? What are the first, small steps on this road? What will demonstrate, in a way that everyone can join, that the journey to the future has begun?

We've reached the end – at least of this cycle – of the company biography. This is a process that can be worked through, somewhat hastily, in a day or can be spread over a much longer period. Whichever way suits your purpose, the company biography activity is worth some investment of your time in order that your plans for the future can be built on a firm understanding of who we are and where we have come from.

Company biography work serves as a foundation for the future in another way. In the past, some companies have commissioned outsiders to write – usually rather eulogistic – company histories. However, just as individual biographies of the past were for the rich and famous, so company histories were restricted to those of the great and good. Now we are in the age when the biography of *every* person is a story worth telling. The biography of every *company* is worth telling, too, as a story of creativity, of development, of collective identity and shared purpose.

5. Era spotting

Some companies make changes, some companies react to changes and some wonder what happened. Which of these categories does your company fall into?

Companies are shaped by and must fit into their era, their time. For companies in the West, this means coming to terms with the decline of the industrial and manufacturing era and getting used to the post-industrial service age. Where the former was dominated by the factory and the demands of production, the latter is more concerned with selling information, image and high-value products and services.

To talk of eras is to talk in vast generalizations. Companies engaged in the extraction of raw materials or in the manufacture of these into products have an important place in the post-industrial society. This term and others like it are descriptions of tendencies, when we seek to put our fingers on the essence and values of the new. Whatever your company makes or does, it has to take into account these new values. Paying attention to operations *inside* the business is a manufacturing era value; looking *outwards* and *onwards* is a keynote of the new. Spotting the era we are in, sensing what it means for the business and trying to anticipate future trends is a vital aspect of Learning Company functioning.

The aim of this chapter is to offer a simple framework for era spotting so that you can build this into the way your company does things so as to ensure that you are always looking inwards, outwards and onwards.

Competitive strategy?

In his analysis of competitive strategy, Porter[1] suggests five forces that can have an impact on any business (Figure 5.1).

These are the traditional factors that people take into account in thinking about their business strategy. These five factors can be more or less easily estimated at any given point in time. However, 'competitive strategy' is necessary but not sufficient. Companies can 'beat' the competition or dominate it for long periods but this is no guarantee of their long-term survival or contribution. Are they really learning anything new? Are they anticipating new requirements or motivations

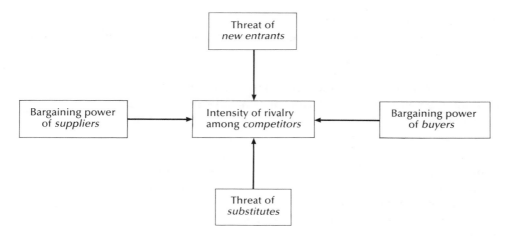

Figure 5.1 The five forces that affect any business

from inside or outside the business? Are they moving on with the era in any significant way?

How can companies pick up the wider, peripheral and often initially nebulous signals that point to the onset of the new? For example, who would have said a few years ago that environmental consciousness would become such a major force that now companies are falling over themselves to be 'green', at least in name? The impact on businesses of this new consciousness is very recent and mainly post-Chernobyl but indications are that many consumers will pay more for 'environmentally friendly' products and avoid others that are seen as potentially harmful to the environment. The usual processes of business modelling, using the notion of competitive strategy, could not have picked this up, yet it is to companies like The Body Shop and Tesco who geared themselves to tackling this issue early, that the main benefits seem to accrue. Others who moved late, reacting to competitors rather than to new, internalized values, probably missed the boat.

Issues in the air

At any one time there are all sorts of issues around getting an airing, so many straws in the wind, so how can we spot the ones that are going to count and move in that direction, rather than have to react to competitive threat later?

Here is a short list of such issues:

- demographic trends – fewer school leavers, proportionally fewer workers, more older and retired people, etc.
- diversity – of people, e.g., sex, age, origins and backgrounds – how can we respect, value and make use of these differences?
- imbalance of rich and poor nations

- the rise of religious fundamentalism
- the increasing importance of business ethics and the lack of these in some businesses
- the rise of world terrorism
- the 'peace dividend' – reduction of arms expenditures
- people demanding fulfilment and personal meaning at work
- green issues
- increased leisure and travel
- instability of world financial markets
- the 'global village' – Europeanization, globalization, etc.
- opening up of the USSR, South Africa, Eastern Europe, China
- collapse of middle management
- drug wars and the economy in North and South America
- women on the board
- representing ethnic minorities in management
- people's increasing demands for development outstripping a company's willingness and ability to provide it
- authoritarianism and the lack of democracy in business
- a move away from unitary organizations towards federal, franchising and networking models
- increasing importance of information and IT in business
- being a socially responsible company, being a good neighbour

. . . and so on. There are many others that would be specific to your business. Which of these, though, should we take notice of and which can we just watch rather than act on? Without a crystal ball you can't be completely sure, but there are processes that you can put in place to make sure you keep looking outwards, inwards and onwards.

A search process

Learning Companies spend time searching and there are many ways of doing this, some of which you will find among the Glimpses in Chapter 7. As a general model, Winter[2] has suggested the following (Figure 5.2):

Here the company values spending some time looking at the long-term and has a leadership that is open to all new information, including, even especially, that which is uncomfortable.

From the data collected and by using Strengths, Weaknesses, Opportunities and Threats (SWOT) analyses and so on, you can create a list of factors or issues in the air for your own company. It is a useful exercise in itself to involve other people in deciding what is likely to be important for the company in the years ahead. When you have a list like the one above, try allocating each of the items to one of three bands:

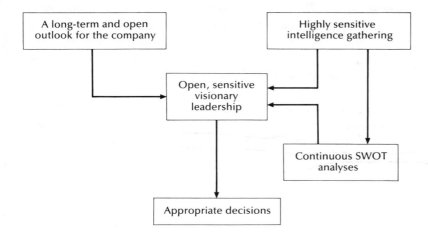

Figure 5.2 Winter's model for the searching process

- band 1 – of central importance now
- band 2 – likely to be of importance in the future; increasing pressure in this direction
- band 3 – still too up in the air to say, keep an eye on this.

We can draw these bands as shown in Figure 5.3 to show these tendencies:

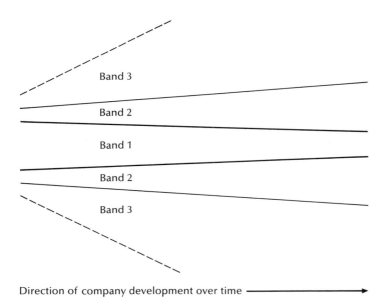

Figure 5.3 Using the results of your SWOT analysis

Band 1 items should be familiar to you and should already be taken account of in existing thinking about the future. Band 2 items are ones that could make all the difference and which you will probably not pick up with normal strategic planning models. Band 3 contains all sorts of weird and wonderful items that are not for action now but are worth keeping a watchful eye on.

A regular search and analysis process will make it more likely that you and your company spot the era you are in. Picking the Band 2 items that are likely to make a difference is the key and a regular process will enable you to see whether any Band 3s move nearer the centre.

REFERENCES

1. Porter, M.E., 'How Competitive Forces Shape Strategy', *Harvard Business Review* (March/April 1979).
2. Winter, R. J., *British Airways and Its Treatment of Peripheral Factors in Strategic Scenarios – A Case of Tunnel Vision?*, MBA Dissertation, University of Lancaster (1990).

This chapter owes much to the original work done by Richard Winter of British Airways.

6. Becoming a Learning Company

Having taken a look at the idea of the Learning Company . . .

. . . having decided that this idea fits in with the aspirations of people in your company . . .

. . . having done some thinking and diagnosis about the aspects of your company that are more developed and less developed in terms of the Learning Company idea . . .

. . . you might now well be asking the question . . .

'How do we get started?'

The aim of this chapter is to offer some starting points for companies wishing to follow a Learning Company strategy.

Given what we have said so far about there being no blueprints and the stress we have put upon the need for transformation to come from within, our basic position is that you can start anywhere that seems possible and appropriate.

To the extent that organizations are organisms, then each small part – every department or section has some capacity to affect the whole of the organization. So, although the Learning Company is a whole organization idea, you can make a start in any part that has the potential to affect the others. The 'Learning Department' might be expected to flourish best in the Learning Company, which might also flourish best in the 'Learning Society' and so on, but we have to start somewhere and why not now? Whatever happens will produce information and learning.

What follows are a number of different starting points for pursuing a Learning Company strategy within your company. These are not mutually exclusive and it is quite likely that you may want to follow more than one or even all of these. Equally, none of these may suit your situation, and you may find your starting point elsewhere. The Learning Company is about aligning and attuning flows of energy so start where the energy is.

- **Work with the board of directors**   In some ways the obvious place to start. Sooner or later these people will have to support and live out the idea in their actions and learning if it is to spread throughout the company. If these people begin to practise the ideas upon themselves and with those with whom they come into contact, then it will have a most powerful effect.
- **Work out from the human resources department**   This starting place has the advantage of being where the people management systems are located. For example, if there is a goal setting and performance review process then the ideas of the Learning Company can be linked into this. People in this function may be relatively knowledgeable about ideas of learning and development. This may help but it may also block a Learning Company initiative.
- **A joint union and management initiative**   In some organizations there is great potential for development in an alliance of managers and trade unionists, working from their respective concerns to challenge and transform existing assumptions and methods of working. As the way we think about organizing becomes more and more crucial to productivity and well-being, so temporary partnerships of old adversaries can often serve to break up old positions and thinking. Any Learning Company initiative in a unionized company must, sooner or later, confront this question of partnership and, rather like human resources depart-ments, trade unions have great potential for supporting *and* for blocking.
- **Set up a series of task forces**   Perhaps task forces could be set up to look at a number of the dimensions of the Learning Company that you wish to pursue. Task forces can function like action learning groups and should have sponsors that they are accountable to and perhaps advisers who can support their work. There could be a 'meta' task force charged with overseeing the whole Learning Company process. As temporary structures, task forces do not threaten the existing power distribution too much and can mobilize large amounts of energy and creativity. Equally they should dissolve themselves when they have accom-plished their goals or when the resistance forces have stopped forward progress.
- **Run a consciousness-raising development programme**   In seeking to 'change their cultures' many organizations have mounted large campaigns that have included significant training courses to get across the message of, for example putting customers first or quality means getting it right every time. This approach must have the Board behind it and can be very effective in the short term for raising energy and expectations. Problems usually occur with the question of what to do afterwards and such an approach needs to be part of a grander strategy?
- **Work with the strategic planning cycle**   In organizations where there is a strong commitment to a cyclical planning process, this might prove to be the right point to attach a Learning Company orientation. The link between planning and learning and the trick of how to look upon planning as learning are crucial factors here. Potentially, the planning process represents a central pivot of organizing on which all members could have a say and make a contribu-tion.

- **Begin with diagnosis** All good organization development interventions begin with data collection, analysis and diagnosis. Our Learning Company profile included in this book is one way of collecting data. We are currently developing a longer, computer-analysed version.

    However, a word of warning – paralysis by analysis is all too common in such approaches and calling for more data is a favourite tactic of the status quo merchants. Another problem is that of being swamped by data because you didn't think carefully and selectively enough about what information to collect. Our inclination is to commission an action learning process that includes the gathering of data as part of taking action and learning from it, and not to split the essential wholeness that is thinking and doing.

- **Start with a community conference or teach in** One way to involve representatives of the whole company in an initial thinking or 'tasting' exercise is to design a conference to introduce people to the idea and to involve them by asking for their opinions about the directions the company should be going in and what problems they foresee in meeting targets and plans. Such conferences can be relatively inexpensive, small steps that none the less produce a lot of enthusiasm and ideas. However, they can suffer from the shortcomings of other 'consciousness raising' approaches unless you have a good commitment to going further.

- **Start with one department** There is no reason why one department should not make a start on the Learning Company process by itself. Supposing the accounts department began to adopt this approach. If they succeeded in changing themselves and the way they worked together then they would eventually 'export' this to the rest of the organization. For example, perhaps there would be a different way of presenting accounts and a different approach to accounting responsibility, together with a new service to internal customers from the department. Obviously there are limits to how far this could go without broader implications, but this could be a very practical place to make a beginning.

- **Major on one of the key dimensions** A company that wished to follow a Learning Company strategy could start by working on one of the dimensions and forget about the others for the time being. For example, the development of a high-quality learning climate or perhaps the spread of informating ideas, technology and software throughout the organization might make good starting places in particular companies. As we have stressed before, our model is only *our* picture of it at this time; it may be a different picture for you and it will certainly change over time. The place to start is where it makes most sense to do so – although always with the big idea, the big picture, at the back of your mind.

7. 101 Glimpses of the Learning Company

The Glimpses in this chapter are not grouped in any particular way and although there are obvious relationships between some of them, no such relationships are implied by the order of presentation. Each Glimpse stands alone, making its own point and this chapter is best thought of as a collection of short stories. Like any such collection, these reflect the underlying themes that preoccupy us, the authors, sometimes individually and often collectively. These themes may, in fact, be a more accurate guide to the future than the specifics of the Glimpses.

There are two guidance systems available for the Glimpses. A complete list of them appears in the Contents at the start of the book and opposite you will find a matrix in which we have attempted to classify the Glimpses by the characteristics of the Learning Company as described in Chapter 2. This is at best a very approximate exercise and you will probably see connections that we haven't and be unable to see connections that we have implied. For those who like maps, though, however unreliable, it provides some starting points.

Matrix – a guide to the Glimpses

Each numbered Glimpse is listed by the characteristics of the Learning Company where it has major and/or minor application. So, if you want to look at all the Glimpses that illuminate informating, for example, you can find them in the matrix and then read the relevant ones.

	Major	Minor
1. A learning approach to strategy	1, 5, 31, 42, 49, 72, 75	33, 39, 48, 51, 54, 66, 76, 77, 78
2. Participative policy-making	6, 16, 17, 32, 33, 34, 35, 40, 54, 57, 72, 92	12, 19, 25, 27, 42, 48, 58, 65, 68, 69, 80, 81, 82, 91
3. Informating	7, 10, 52, 74, 77, 78, 79, 88, 95	53, 59
4. Formative accounting and control	8, 11, 53, 85, 86	10, 19, 28, 52, 92
5. Internal exchange	18, 25, 40, 61, 73, 74	6, 9, 16, 34, 35, 54, 68, 71, 85, 86
6. Reward flexibility	80, 85, 86, 100	
7. Enabling structures	2, 9, 13, 15, 19, 20, 21, 26, 28, 30, 43, 64, 71	6, 11, 16, 18, 21, 36, 45, 46, 47, 65, 70, 73, 74, 77, 78, 79, 89
8. Boundary workers as environmental scanners	12, 29, 50, 53, 101	31, 66, 79, 90
9. Inter-company learning	17, 25, 30, 37, 48, 49, 55, 56, 66, 93	3, 20, 50, 79, 82, 91, 98
10. Learning climate	14, 22, 23, 24, 43, 44, 54, 62, 63, 74, 76, 87	2, 3, 4, 9, 10, 18, 21, 36, 40, 45, 46, 47, 64, 65, 71, 73, 79, 94
11. Self-development for all	3, 4, 11, 21, 27, 36, 45, 46, 47, 73, 80, 81, 82, 89, 91, 94, 97	2, 7, 16, 18, 24, 43, 61, 71, 74
Overview	34, 38, 39, 41, 51, 53, 58, 59, 60, 65, 67, 68, 69, 83, 84, 96, 98, 99	13, 29, 49, 70, 72

Glimpse 1
The management challenge

Challenging your own norms and assumptions is difficult. As the terms imply, these everyday structures of individual and corporate lives are taken for granted, not noticed, in effect, invisible to those who follow or hold them. They are much more obvious to others who follow different norms and assumptions who, while similarly blind to their own taken for granted norms and assumptions, can ask penetrating and provoking questions about those of others.

Royal Dutch Shell have tried to incorporate this potentially valuable process into their company operations with what they call 'the management challenge'. Every three years, a senior executive from another plant, and usually another country, visits a given location to deliver a challenge to management. He or she spends a week or so at the site, wandering around, reading reports, talking to people before challenging the managing team. The challenge itself involves presenting observations, impressions, making suggestions but, above all, asking 'naive' questions, questions that an insider would not ask because the answers are obvious. These questions are basically of the nature 'Why do you do such and such?' or 'How does this and that contribute to plant efficiency?' The local managers must publish the challenge and their responses to it.

The management challenge is one way of ensuring that the 'hidden' fundamentals of 'how we do things round here' are questioned on a regular basis. Such questioning seems to be an essential component of 'double loop learning' or the reframing essential to organizational transformation. You could institute your own management challenge and put in place this vital aspect of organizational learning by inviting different people in to question your operations. Why not start by inviting fellow managers from a sister plant? If you feel up to being more challenged than this you could invite a customer, a supplier or a stakeholder from the local community.

Glimpse 2
The developing centre

Alistair Crombie suggests that the cultivation of the Learning Company can be helped by a centre within an organization that promotes enquiry and learning throughout it. The mission of the centre is *not* to put on courses (although it might run a few), but to research, animate and facilitate individual and organizational learning. The centre is autonomous, reports to the CEO, has a committed core team on three-year contracts and is guided by an advisory board drawn from both inside and outside the organization.

In Swindon in the UK, Thorn EMI established the Development Centre in 1985 with the mission:

> . . . to contribute to the long-term competitive advantage of Thorn Home Electronics International Ltd (THEI) businesses through the effective enhancement of individual and collective learning and development.

The centre's principles include promoting learning as a way of life and addressing the questions of long-term cultural change. Clear beliefs underlie these principles. Among these is that change starts with the person and that those who prescribe change for others while not practising it personally are unlikely to influence others in developing themselves and the business. At a collective level, cultural change is likely to come about if ideas and experience are shared across businesses in Thorn.

Thorn's managers are encouraged to use the development centre as a 'drop in', to do some individual work, to bring their people for an 'away day' or to talk over business and personal development issues. It took some time to create a healthy relationship between the centre and its 'customers'. People's expectations sometimes led them to demand courses and programmes and they found it hard to understand why these were not forthcoming. The Development Centre disbanded in 1989.

REFERENCE

Crombie, A., 'In Search of the Learning Organization', *Human Futures* (Spring 1981).

Glimpse 3
A learning ladder

Worries about future shortages of young people led Express Foods in the UK to set up a learning ladder that offers a variety of programmes, starting with adult literacy and culminating in an MBA degree. The reasoning behind the scheme is that future job seekers will be in a 'buyer's market' and will choose employers who offer development opportunities as well as decent pay and conditions.

The personnel director, who developed the learning ladder, spent a year thinking about the idea before he started to talk to his fellow directors. He attended seminars and read books about likely future demographic changes and the emergence of more flexible, adaptable organizations. He took time to talk personally to all his colleagues before tabling the idea. He felt it was crucially important not only to allow it to 'ferment' properly but also to arrive at the form most appropriate to the business.

Express Foods' learning ladder is being put into place over five or six years. This amount of time is necessary to create the infrastructure to support it. For example, an underlying principle is that line managers are responsible for the training and development of their people, therefore, to enable the scheme to work well, all managers are being offered the opportunity to practise their skills as coaches, counsellors and mentors.

The personnel director chose a local business school to be the company's collaborating partner. The teaching and academic assessment are carried out by the business school, but it is the line managers who will bear the crucial responsibility for ensuring that what individuals learn is welcomed and brought back into the business. One of the personnel director's selling points to his colleagues was that not only will the scheme attract young people and encourage all company personnel to develop further, but that once people have a foot on a rung, they will want to climb higher.

The learning ladder will not only bring people in, it will keep them in.

The 'tied cottage' approach to management development

In some organizations management development has been seen as a reward to individuals rather than as an investment by the business. Like other rewards and benefits, such as pay, share options, pension and health schemes, provision of company cars and dining room facilities, management development opportunities have varied according to one's place in the hierarchy. For example, one large company sends

- its directors to the Harvard Business School
- its senior managers to the London Business School
- its middle managers to the local polytechnic
- its supervisors to the local college.

While management development is restricted to the above, other ranks have in-company training as appropriate. This company regards itself, and is regarded in the industry, as following best practice and putting a lot of effort into training and development activities. The 'tied cottage' approach – what you get depends on your status, and perhaps, behave yourself if you want to continue to get it – however, looks old-fashioned in contrast to some more recent thinking.

An introductory letter to a new management development information pack from the BBC includes the paragraph:

> Fourth, and most important, management training is available not simply for line managers, but for anyone with a management component in their job. In practice this means most of us. We all have to manage our time, our priorities, the resources we use, our colleagues, or our boss.

Management development in the Learning Company is for everyone who uses resources to get the job done.

Glimpse 5
A vision of Chrystal Computing – a play in two acts

Despite a string of locally celebrated people down the ages, clairvoyance still has some way to go before it will be found in the average company planner's tool kit. Envisioning is another matter.

Mike Summers is the junior partner in Chrystal Computing, a software house with some 30 full- and part-time staff. His fellow partners, Dennis the marketing supremo and Diane the technical wizard, brought Mike in as much for his background in business planning as his systems experience. After a year in the company, Mike is feeling well established enough, and clear enough about some of the problems to be able to think about a development plan for the business. To help him get a clearer vision of what he'd like to see in the future, he has enlisted the help of Tom, a consultant, who he has worked with before.

Act 1

Tom   So start by telling me about the business . . .

Mike   OK. Well I need to start with Dennis who acts like the owner, although Diane has as much equity. He's an unusual guy – a technical specialist who really likes owning and running the business, an opportunist and a good marketeer. He intervenes a lot and loves changing things. Diane is quieter, more straightforward, she gets her satisfaction from product development. Let's see, turnover is £3 million and rising, products are mainly bespoke open and distance learning packages for clients, new areas of great interest are expert systems for learning resources centres in large organizations and also networking infrastructures for dispersed businesses. A big worry is that we need to increase our client base, three quarters of our turnover comes from two big clients who could switch direction or move to a competitor at any time.

Tom   Yes, I think I'm getting a picture – tell me what it feels like.

Mike   Well, as I've said, Dennis really enjoys running the business and making things happen. If I've got a client in my office, he'll come in and meet and invite them to lunch, then I tag along even though it's *my* client. It's not just me, he does this with everyone.

There's a feeling that you have to get Dennis' attention if you want to change things, even quite small ones. This is not very empowering either for the consultants or for the support staff – except for Dennis!

There are two cultures really – the Diane culture is all hi-tech, very tasky, clear, long-term plans and tight controls; the Dennis culture is more people-centred, relationships are important, especially with clients, you follow the people and the mood, much less control.

Tom   Is it light or dark? Fast or slow? Fun or serious?

Mike   It's fast, under-resourced, we're mainly too busy. It's light, people like each other and know each other well, there's a good sense of humour and of play, bits of larking about. Quite often we'll open a bottle – those of us who are there after six. Hard-working but not much of a feeling of progress, a certain feeling of stuckness.

Tom   About what?

Mike   I don't know . . . products? We're not very clear about what we do collectively. People work on their own projects, no one has much of an overview apart from me and Dennis. Also that we have too few clients, it's too precarious, and yet people don't know what to do about that.

Tom   OK. What's the office like, the furniture, the clothes?

Mike   It's in the town centre, on the fourth floor in an old office block with a shared receptionist on the ground floor. It's rather cramped but comfortable with lots of plants and the coffee pot always full. There's just enough room in my office for me and one client. Furniture is a mixture of ancient and modern – old desks, folding Italian chairs – I like it. Clothes are casual to smart – people wear suits to talk to clients but not your pinstripes.

Tom   When you reach the office in the morning, are you looking forward to the day?

Mike   Most of the time. Yes, when I'm well stuck into a project; no, when I don't know what I should be doing or whether I should be looking for new business.

Tom   What about pay, hours, etc?

Mike   Support workers get straight salaries, while consultants' pay is either salary plus job-related bonuses or fees for part-timers. Hours are longish – 9.30 to anytime really.

Mike and Tom continue their conversation on similar lines. Tom prompting, Mike filling in the details of his 'now' picture.

Act 2

Tom   Right. So now tell me what it looks like three years hence.

Mike   Well, turnover has gone up to say £6 million, we have a dozen new clients, we've moved into new fields, new products, I don't know, this is difficult.

Tom   Yes, I know, but keep trying – what's the office like?

Mike   We've moved into new premises, bigger and out of the town centre, we have our own receptionist who makes clients feel at home, who makes people enjoy visiting us. I have a lot more space in my office, the furniture is a bit smarter, more modern, we have more technology than ever but also areas to sit down in and have discussions over coffee with nice chairs and views from the window. There's a lot more colour about. There's a 'drop in' feel to the place. Clients come in quite casually and if the person they want to see is not in we know where they are and can get in touch by phone or with our new viewphone.

Tom   Good. What's Dennis doing?

Mike   He's signing cheques and taking a client out to lunch – but it's *his* client, not mine. I'm going to take mine out later. Dennis has learned to delegate more and also to ask people for their ideas and listen to what they say. He's still full of ideas and energy but now he can say to someone 'That's a good idea, why don't you get on with it' instead of rushing off to do it himself. Oh yes!

Tom   What?

Mike   We have a business mission statement that has been put together after a series of meetings involving all the staff, including part-timers and support staff. People were reluctant to voice their views until they'd heard from Dennis, but I nobbled him beforehand, so he didn't say too much at once. Now we've done this one it will be easier next time.

Tom   How about the people?

Mike   Happier – just as busy but clearer about roles and responsibilities; we have more formal roles now with project managers and so on. Numbers are about the same by the way, but we put out more and we have a lot more women, maybe 60:40 men:women. Some of the new consultants are ex support staff who have been encouraged to develop themselves. We put in individual development plans for *all* staff that are reviewed six-monthly – that's my job, and this includes Dennis. As part of this review, each member of staff has to get the views of at least two other people as to how they're doing and what they should be doing next. The reward system encourages people to move up and take on more skills and responsibilities. For instance, when we put on a new support worker they are given a clear understanding that if they want to progress into consultancy and have the ability and commitment, then we will help them and train them to do so. We have lost a few of our consultants, but not to competitors except in the sense that they've gone freelance and *become* competitors. We keep in touch with them, do business with them still.

Tom   Sounds good. Does Dennis still do all the selling?

Mike   No. Consultants are encouraged to be more entrepreneurial, to seek out new clients and new products, but they can't go ahead without proposing to our fortnightly business planning meeting where we review progress and OK new projects.

Tom   Who runs this meeting?

Mike   We rotate the chair as a learning experience. All staff can attend, although usually we have 12 or 15 and I often have to chivvy some to turn up, especially the old hands. This meeting is really the decision forum for the whole business. Of course, Dennis could veto anything he really didn't like, but so far the most that has happened is for proposals to go back for more work. Anything crazy we'd try to talk out beforehand.

Tom   What's the downside in this paradise?

Mike   Ah, well, maybe some people are working too hard? Some stress around? We are so successful in what we do that we are beginning to attract predators – Dennis might be tempted to sell out soon. As the excitement of building the new business wears off – we've stabilized in numbers of people at least and put some useful systems into place – people are looking for something new. What's next?

Glimpse 6
Learning from dialectic

Many managerial problems turn out to be messy and poorly defined. It is sometimes hard to tell the problem from the symptoms or to pick out the relevant information from the vast mass available. Matters seem to be full of contradictions and paradoxes. There are different values among members that lead to political and emotional clashes.

The stresses of managing ambiguity are enormous. In such situations we are tempted to go for 'quick fixes' or to contain the conflict and mess in some way – if only for the sake of our own health. Learning Companies have to do better than this. Conflict is stressful but it is also a source of creativity, of testing old ideas and generating new ones. An organization that structures out conflict will also cut out challenge, risk, creativity and learning.

Michael McCaskey describes a way of using three groups taken from the organization to conduct a dialectic in order to try to get the benefits of conflict without the destruction.

- Three groups, A, B and C, are set up to tackle an agreed problem area. The most senior person is put into Group C.
- Group A goes off and develops an analysis and a plan for action on the problem using any agreed method.
- A's list of key assumptions is then turned over to Group B that has the job of preparing counter-assumptions and an antithesis to A's plan.
- Next, Group C facilitates a structured debate. A & B take turns to give spirited presentations, outlining their assumptions and the key data that they consider of importance. Each then probes the weaknesses in each other's plans using wit and humour as well as logic and analysis. A sense of the dramatic is helpful here. The facilitator(s) must work to balance combativeness with goodwill and prevent personal attacks. The rest of Group C note significant points and omissions.
- Once the arguments begin to be repeated, the facilitator ends the debate and calls a break for members to socialize and re-connect at a personal level.
- Then the whole conference, led by members of Group C, generates a list of agreed assumptions, a set of key data and a plan for action.

This harnessing of the dialectic can lead to a constructive use of conflict. It can bring to the surface existing differences, tensions and values. The clash of views can create something new – a third position from the opposing two – that may contain aspects of both together with higher validity or acceptability than either. It is a good way to test a plan and a method for involving more people and more parts of the organization in policy making.

REFERENCE

Michael McCaskey, 'The Challenge of Managing Ambiguity and Change' in Pondy, Boland & Thomas (eds), *Managing Ambiguity and Change*, Wiley (1988).

Glimpse 7
Working in the electronic learning net

Computer Mediated Communications Systems (CMCS) exploit the storage, processing and retrieval capabilities of the company mainframe for internal and external communications. Database, texts, articles, reports, manuals, directories and so on can be held for quick and easy access by members. Communications software including EMail, Bulletin Boards and Conferencing allows for interaction between members both person-to-person and among dispersed groups. CMCS provides an electronic learning environment where all members have equal access to data and are able to communicate freely.

Any member can take part and all the company PC's are networked through the mainframe with relevant external systems. Thus remote access to national and international knowledge networks are available within the company at any time. CMCS is increasingly being used to deliver all kinds of education and training programmes in which users typically report higher levels of interest, involvement and personal control than with conventional delivery methods. CMCS also provide for the distributed knowledge networks that are at the heart of up-to-date professional practice sometimes known as Executive Information Systems (EIS).

Helen James works for a large international firm of consulting engineers as an internal management advisor. She is currently involved with an important project team that is advising on the building of an integrated steel plant in the USSR.

As part of her work with the project team Helen puts out regular progress reports of the project on the internal network Bulletin Board. On arriving at work on Monday she finds various EMail items from the weekend. One is from a manager in new product development asking for details of the project planning methods being used. Another is a request from an engineer for a short attachment for personal learning purposes with the project team. Helen prints these off to present to her project team meeting later in the week.

Helen also belongs to a professional association and has been taking part in an on-line seminar on new organizational structures. This morning she logs into the seminar and finds that since she last took part several members have been exchanging ideas about temporary structures and 'opportunity structures'. After scanning the summaries, she downloads the full texts for later study. Meanwhile she makes some notes and prepares some questions to add to the discussion section of the conference later on. She then logs into the Papernet held by her association to see whether there are any items relevant to the steel plant project. She notes the names and numbers of two members offering papers on project management and cross-cultural issues to follow up later. Finally, before going to her 10.00 a.m. meeting she sends travel warrant requests and last month's expenses through to the relevant section via EMail.

Returning some two hours later, Helen deals with a query about her travel requirements before logging on again and instructing her PC to send the previously noted comments to the Organizational Structures Conference and to send requests for the Papernet offerings. She has also received an invitation from Vienna to contribute to an electronic journal on managing in a unified Europe that addresses comparisons and contrasts between western and eastern approaches. She makes notes in her computer diary to remind her to clear some papers on the USSR project with the project team before offering them to the journal.

FOLLOW-UP READING

McConnell, D. and V. Hodgson, 'Computer Mediated Communications Systems (CMCS) – Electronic Networking and Education', *Management Education & Development*, 21(1) (Spring 1990).

Glimpse 8
Accounting roadshows at Mercian Windows

Following several requests after a series of customer care programmes, the finance department at Mercian Windows set up a roadshow to go at fairly short notice to any of the 38 branch offices of the company. As an operationally decentralized but financially centralized organization, Mercian Windows needed to ensure that branch management teams understood the way money worked in the company in order to make better business deals and, in particular, to take appropriate risks.

The roadshow consists of the branch accountant from head office, the factory accountant, the internal auditor and an attached management trainee. The roadshow includes a video, some short presentations, self-development activities, designed to illustrate the workings of the money system, and opportunities for personal one-to-one or small group coaching to work through specific issues. In addition, and following a roadshow visit, branch managers are encouraged to set up a further learning contract with the head office which can involve further study, visits and contacts.

The accounting roadshow has certainly shown head office to be responsive and resulted in some branch managers being better informed. In the Learning Company we would ask a further question – 'Has it resulted in any changes to the way finance is done in the company?' The finance director was cautious on this point, saying 'It has certainly resulted in changes to the way we present financial information in the company' – this was as far as he would go.

Glimpse 9
Creating headroom

Making the right sort of space for development – physical, social and psychological – is an essential task for all organizational 'architects' who are interested in creating the Learning Company. Noisy manufacturing processes, over-controlled hierarchies and crowded premises can all block the opportunities for risk and reflection needed for learning. Making room for development is an aspect of building enabling rather than disabling structures.

'Shifting the deckchairs on the Titanic' is the modern managerial equivalent of 'fiddling while Rome burns'. However, small steps can often be the most effective. Distinguishing the fertile from the futile can be difficult, particularly from the outside, where the meaning of a given gesture is not always apparent.

At Wisewood School in Sheffield, the headteacher, his three deputies and two senior teachers act together and think of themselves as a team. They wanted to demonstrate this and to make a strong and clear statement about this way of managing. They decided to move out of their separate offices and share one room. This met a secondary objective of releasing five rooms for other purposes.

What the senior management team had not anticipated was the knock-on effects of their action. They began to notice small and incremental changes in the positioning of furniture and work spaces taking place all over the school. Bookcases, previously used as screens, were put against walls; filing cabinets used to block the view and create privacy were moved out of the way. A ripple effect of the teams' actions seemed to spread throughout the school. The overall impression was of taking down barriers and opening access and communications. The five offices previously filled by the senior teachers became much needed private interview and meeting rooms used on a bookable basis.

Glimpse 10
The informated paper mill

Beetham Paper Mill in Lancashire boasts a very special and expensive piece of equipment. It can make an unusually wide range of products, can be reset easily to different specifications and therefore has a great ability to meet customers' urgent small batch demands. However, the catch is that if the machine does not reach quality standards, then the economic consequences are dire. You can't afford the wastage that is normal on the slow learning curve of a long run standard product.

This was a major problem for operators as they tried to check the quality specifications early in each new batch. It took several minutes to go round all the dials and gauges in order to make adjustments. Then the company installed new monitoring equipment that gives an instant digital display of the quality and specification of the paper coming off the machine. This step cut waste to negligible proportions but also dramatically changes the experience of the operators. They can now see the effects of adjustments as they make them. Interestingly, the monitors keep a cumulative score of quality output as well as current data – they say it's like playing space invaders.

This is a simple illustration of the rewards that can come – in both financial and quality of working life terms – from applying information technology to provide feedback for quick learning, greater productivity and job satisfaction.

Glimpse 11
Personal development budgets

A National Health Service development programme for unit general managers includes £300 for each individual to spend as they wish. They can use it to buy books, to make visits, to buy in expertise, to go on a seminar. This is a very concrete way to empower learners and can produce self-management pay-offs out of all proportion to the smallish sums of cash involved.

The idea of personal development budgets is spreading in companies who want to step up their learning. There is nothing that demonstrates commitment to self-development more than giving a small but no-strings-attached cash budget to individuals. One company has divided its whole training budget by the number of staff and given complete responsibility for spending to individuals.

Many people are very parsimonious with their budgets, finding very economical ways to support their learning and often pooling with others to put on special events or opportunities. These budgets can lead people not only to looking for value for money but also to breaking out of the habit of thinking, 'if it's learning it must be a course'. They can stimulate a lot of careful thought about learning and development needs – not only by the individual but also by their manager.

Some companies have systems that require submission of plans for approval to managers or committees before the budget can be spent, but it is very easy to kill interest and motivation by introducing such controls. Most people spend their budgets wisely and the problem can be getting some to spend their budgets in time. It is better to give people total control and responsibility for managing themselves and then create opportunities to review learning and development on occasions such as annual appraisals.

Glimpse 12
Environmental scanning at Harvest Bakeries

At Harvest Bakeries, everyone with a 'boundary role' – one with working contacts outside the company – is expected to pick up useful information and bring it back. Marketing people are used to doing this, but now the delivery people enquire about complaints and ask supermarket managers what new products they would like to see Harvest Bakeries offer. This information is pooled at weekly debriefing meetings and the bonus system rewards named individuals for useful ideas.

Many companies spend a good deal of money on market research to find out things their people already know or could easily find out. To make your boundary workers into environmental scanners means convincing them that this is important and worthwhile. The system for collecting and using the information is vital and it helps to be able to recognize and reward the effort people put in. Using your people as intelligence gatherers could really open your eyes.

Glimpse 13
The fourth dimension of structure

Tom Lupton has suggested that designing a company is a bit like doing a three-sided Rubik Cube – there are three 'logics' to get right all at once.

- **Technical logic** means that things have to facilitate the work flow to produce goods and services. This includes the production process, the delivery of supplies and the despatch of finished goods or, in the case of a service, the logical steps to deliver that service to the customer. Material and information flow between work units and departments have to be arranged in the best pattern.
- **Financial logic** means that the costs incurred and the value added at each stage of production have to be arranged to maximize income and minimize cost. As we know, financial logic is often different from technical, and both can be very different from the third type of logic, human.
- **Human logic** decrees that work has to be arranged so that it is possible for people to do it – jobs defined and linked, people selected and trained with the appropriate skills, and the right working conditions established. The effort/reward equation has to be right in the short and long term to match the labour market and meet people's expectations for money, variety, career progression.

These three logics go into the structuring of companies, which can be quite tightly designed and controlled. Indeed, mature companies are often so 'tight' that they can become rigid and inflexible, lacking that element of novelty or randomness that can lead to change and learning.

The Learning Company has a fourth logic – a **learning logic** which allows people, individually and as a company, to flow, adapt, change and develop. This means that those previously tight logics – technical, financial and human – have to flex to allow for learning. There are many glimpses in this book of flexible adaptive structures, systems and procedures. The Learning Company is one that incorporates this fourth dimension of structure – the logic of learning.

Glimpse 14
The Learning Company litmus test?

What is the reaction to failure in your company? Do people deny their mistakes, bury the evidence and cover their backs? Or do they say, 'I did it like this and it didn't work, but this is what I learned from it'?

The Learning Company strives to create this latter kind of climate where failures, accidents, breakdowns and mistakes are learned from so that they can be avoided in the future. This means making time for review, whatever the work pressures. It means that the leadership style and culture is about learning from experience and not one of allocating blame and punishment. Managers say things like, 'Do your best and if it doesn't work, let's talk about it and find out why'. Planning to collect information, to monitor, review and evaluate new ventures is part of the skill of operating the Learning Company.

This doesn't mean that we *choose* failure or take stupid risks – far from it. If you want a litmus paper test of where your company stands as a Learning Company, just look at the way the last three errors, breakdowns or failures were dealt with.

- Did people talk openly about them or did they hide away and avoid the subject?
- What was learned from the mistakes?
- Did people get blamed or did they feel empowered as a result of the post-mortem?

In non-Learning Companies it just isn't possible to talk about mistakes. If you make one you feel awful about it, it gets left with you, it isn't on to talk about it and redeem the error through learning and the knowledge that things will be different next time.

As ever, the Learning Company starts with little things. You can make a start today by talking about failure in a constructive spirit. Adopting a non-punitive – but not soft – leadership style is something any one person can do today to move us all that little bit along the road to becoming a Learning Company.

Glimpse 15
Whither middle management?

The IT and TQM 'revolutions' are creating havoc for the middle management role by taking over many of the traditional functions of information collection, coordination of activities and mediating between operational and strategic management. Some TQM programmes have led to internal work units treating each other as buyers and suppliers, monitoring quality, quantity, time and cost factors and removing the need for middle men to communicate and arbitrate between them.

The trend is clear, though it varies greatly by industry and sector. Many companies are simply doing away with great swathes of middle managers. Some may be concerned to have some of its erstwhile middle managers playing a key part in the core processes of the Learning Company. Who else is processing alternative visions of current operating arrangements? Who can shape up options for strategic evaluation and plan detailed implementation procedures? In this second scenario, middle managers' prime concerns could become business development, human resource development and the facilitation of change in operations.

FOLLOW-UP READING

Drucker, P. F., 'The Coming of the New Organization', *Harvard Business Review* (January/ February 1988).

Glimpse 16
Search conferencing

Participative policy making means getting more rather than fewer people involved in discussing and deciding on the goals, strategies, policies and procedures of the organization. One of the excuses for not extending policy making beyond the 'big boys' at the top is that of practicality – how do you involve everyone in making decisions?

A good question and one that is addressed by the idea of the 'search conference'. Originated by Fred Emery as a methodology for collaborative ecological planning, this is a process for searching possible futures and generating desirable strategies for action. In 'social island' conditions – that is isolated away from work and home – search conferences proceed by a mixture of plenary and small task group sessions. They always work with future, past and present, with the firm rule that whatever the sequence of the first two, the present is always dealt with last. In terms of values, the search conference 'is an expression of participatory democracy, and seeks to lead individuals and groups in the direction of greater purposefulness and enhanced self-management' (Crombie 1985). Search conferences can operate on behalf of quite big communities – Herbst (1978) gives an example from northern Norway where a community of 3600 people sent representatives to a two-day conference to decide on plans for the future of the community.

Here is a design for a two-day search conference of 30 people representing a hotel chain with 2700 employees. The theme was 'Attracting, Keeping and Developing Our People'. Briefly, this is what happens during the course of the search conference.

Five or six groups are invited to represent the main stakeholders in the organizational community, in this case, for example:

- owners and managers
- customers, individual and corporate
- staff group from small hotels
- catering and housekeeping staff
- community representatives, e.g., suppliers, local government planners and economic development officers, school careers staff

- new staff joining within the last six months.

The two days, held in a university hall of residence, are chaired and facilitated by two consultants responsible for the structure but not the content of the sessions.

The search conference moves in two directions:

- divergent – identifying the range of desired goals and present problems
- convergent – clarifying and prioritizing problems and seeking lines of collaborative action.

On Day 1, in *homogeneous* groups, people work in the morning on the questions 'What major changes have taken place in the company from the past until the present?' and 'Are these positive or negative?' Following a plenary before lunch to collect data on work so far, in the afternoon they look at the questions 'What changes do you expect in the future?' and 'Are these positive or negative?'

On Day 2, in *heterogeneous* groups – the representative groups are now mixed – people work on clarifying problems; then meet in plenary to negotiate an agreed list of priorities before returning to small groups to prepare strategies of practical action for each of the chosen problems.

A final plenary session agrees several proposals for action and refers two that involve considerable expense to the Board of Directors. The Personnel Director gets the job of establishing task forces to be responsible for planning and executing the agreed changes.

Also, most importantly, the conference decides on what and how to report back to the other members of the organization. Apart from the agreed list of actions, it is agreed that one person in each of the groups will write ten lines on their personal experience of the search conference and that one of the consultants will include these in a short account of the conference's purposes, methods of working and results to be published in the company newspaper.

REFERENCES

Crombie, A., 'The Nature and Types of Search Conferences', *International Journal of Life-long Education*, 4(1), pages 3–33 (1985).
Herbst, P. G., *Community Conference Design: Skjervoy Yesterday, Today and Tomorrow*, Work Research Institute (1978).

Glimpse 17
The good company

Is a Learning Company a *good* company? When Peters and Waterman produced a list of 'excellent' companies in their book *In Search of Excellence* (Harper & Row, 1982), they were criticized among other things for using financial performance or profit as the sole criterion of 'excellence'. By this definition, it doesn't count if a company pays low wages and provides poor working conditions for employees; it doesn't matter whether its operations damage the environment or that it uses its buying power to force its suppliers' prices down in poor countries. In fact, on financial performance alone, doing these things would make it an even *more* 'excellent' company.

We know that many of our best-known firms engage in business practices that they would rather we didn't know about. It took the loss of a major share of the student market to force a certain British bank to disengage from South Africa, for example. Other companies making cigarettes or nuclear power or chemicals not only turn a blind eye to research findings for years, but also actively seek to have the research stopped or, at the very least, to overcome such findings by heavy counter-advertising.

'That's business' we say. For some people 'business' and ethical values belong to different worlds. Business in the week and ethics on Sundays? This isn't good enough. Our businesses exert enormous influence over the shape of our lives and of our social and natural environments. We need good businesses to create a better world.

Total Quality Management (TQM) means more than just good products, a good working environment and respect for customers. A company really committed to Total Quality is continuously striving for a better quality for *all stakeholders* – of service to customers, of working life for employees, of investment to shareholders and of being a good neighbour and citizen in the wider community.

So, is a Learning Company also a *good* company? Possibly. Is a Learning Company *automatically* a good company? Almost certainly not. A company could be developing along the lines of our model and still be pursuing anti-social ends. A good company is one that strives to be aware of all its possible stakeholders and their needs and to balance these against its own needs to survive and develop.

Where would you place your company on the grid in Figure G17.1?

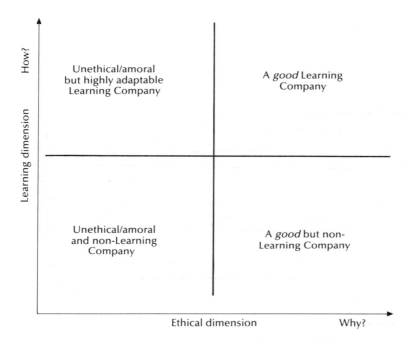

Figure G17.1 Finding out where a company stands on ethical and learning fronts

REFERENCE

Morris, J., 'Good Company' in *Management Education & Development*, 18(2), pages 103–115 (1987).

Glimpse 18
Self and Peer Assessment (SAPA)

The Learning Company is flatter in hierarchical terms than its predecessors: we are professionals and co-workers for the most part. The Learning Company relies less on line management and more on individual responsibility, autonomy and decision making. The ideas of accountability and appraisal are important in all organizations to make sure that we all aim towards common goals. However, as we know, appraisal systems usually don't work because they are done by 'bosses' to 'subordinates' and so are more about dishing out merit awards or apportioning blame than they ever are about development and learning from actions at work.

SAPA is an essential tool in Learning Companies. The process is simple to map out but requires considerable self and peer skills to do. However skilful you are, it won't work without the right learning climate. Here is a step-by-step process you could try out with your colleagues.

- Invite a group of colleagues to join you in experimenting with SAPA.
- Each person chooses one or more areas of task responsibility on which they wish to improve their performance.
- The group brainstorms a list of criteria for all the areas of performance chosen by members.
- Each person chooses criteria from this list and makes a private assessment of their performance against them. (Try using both a qualitative description *and* a quantitative rating. However much you might want to escape from memories of the classroom, giving yourself four out of ten for a performance does rather concentrate the mind! Colleagues should have the right *not* to give marks if they don't wish to.)
- Each person then chooses some peer assessors. This can be the whole group, if it is small enough, or it may be one or two people. (Do you choose your friends or your critics?)
- In the meeting with their chosen peers, each person gives their own assessment of their own performance and asks for questions, feedback and suggestions for improvement. (You're in charge and you choose what you want back. If you want the naked truth then you will have to say so, and perhaps go to some lengths to persuade people that it's safe to be honest with you. If you can't take the whole truth that morning then say so.)

• Before their time is up, each person commits themselves to a line of action and a review date with named peers.

If you wish, and if you have the support of all concerned for doing so, you can have a system of reporting to the centre, whereby members log their improvement plans and report progress over time. This can be private or open to inspection, but if it ever becomes used for control purposes without each person's consent then the system will soon decay and become lifeless.

In the British National Health Service 'Clinical Audit' is the method chosen for encouraging doctors to learn with and from their colleagues. It takes time as it is not easy raising questions of personal security and professional ethics and it is quite a different process to a normal appraisal. SAPA is not mutually exclusive with appraisal and you might be able to run both systems side by side.

SAPA is arguably a better way for professionals to collaborate on performance review. Its greatest strength is that it focuses on learning and performance improvement via learner control and self-direction.

FOLLOW-UP READING

Heron, J., 'Self and Peer Assessment' in T. Boydell and M. Pedler, *Management Self-development: Concepts and Practices*, Gower (1981).

Glimpse 19
Ackoff's circular organization

Russell Ackoff has suggested that all people in authority in organizations, from the chief executive to the supervisor, should have boards made up of their immediate superiors and subordinates to create a circularity of responsibility and accountability. He also advocates that, where they are recognized, trade unions join the boards at all levels. These boards are responsible for planning and coordinating the work for which that person is responsible and also for reviewing and evaluating his or her performance. The board have considerable powers, including that of recommending the removal of the person from office.

In Figure G19.1 people at various levels of authority are shown by the numbers 1 to 4; complete lines show the authority relationships and the dotted ones show board membership:

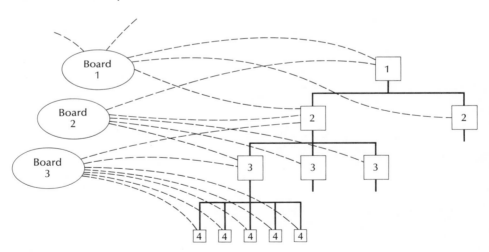

Figure G19.1 Ackoff's circular organization

Ackoff claims over ten years' experience with the circular organization in companies as diverse as Kodak, Alcoa, Anheuser-Busch and A & P Supermarkets. He stresses that the precise form varies from organization to organization, but that the evidence is that organizational democracy and operating efficiency go together.

The circular organization addresses three major organizational needs to increase:

- organizational democracy
- the readiness, willingness and ability of people in the organization to change
- the quality of working life in the organization via participation in managing at all levels.

REFERENCES AND FOLLOW-UP READING

Ackoff, R., *Creating the Corporate Future*, John Wiley (1981).

Ackoff, R., 'The Circular Organization: An Update' in *The Academy of Management Executive*, 3(1), pages 11–16 (1989).

Glimpse 20
Scaffolding

One of the critical dimensions of the Learning Company is the provision of enabling structures. Structures can be

- *physical* like buildings, offices, room layouts
- *procedural* like policy statements, action plans, training schemes
- *mental and cultural* structures of 'how we do things around here', what is done and what is not, what is taken for granted and so on.

One of the key managerial skills in the Learning Company is the ability to create enabling rather than disabling structures. The aim of the Learning Company is to do away with restrictive job descriptions, over-controlled hierarchies, red tape procedures and rigid mind sets that continue unproductive practice indefinitely.

The idea of scaffolding can help refurbish old structures. Don't tear them down and put up the first thing that comes into your head – that's how we got those speculative office buildings we all complain about. Scaffolding is something you erect around an existing structure so that the necessary building or re-building can be done. Scaffolding is a *temporary structure* that is not the change itself. In trying to bring about changes it is very useful to have such a temporary structure to enable those involved in the change to have access to the familiar and to hold things together until the change is completed. So, you *don't* have to go straight from old to new, you can use temporary scaffolding around a difficult or contentious change that allows for the debate, discussion and revision of plans necessary before you commit yourselves irrevocably to a new system or structure.

In the Learning Company, dedicated as it is to learning, adaptation and flexibility, it may be that most structures are temporary and seen as such by people in the company. Scaffolding can also help in setting up joint ventures with other companies where such partnerships can be risky. We can dismantle and move them about any time we like, but, at the same time, they have to be strong enough to take the weight and strain of company operations as well as reassure us all that the structure itself is safe and sound.

Glimpse 21
Spacemaking

Before people can take initiatives, either for their own development or for the development of the business, certain conditions are necessary. Perhaps the most important conditions are those of time and space – we need them both for development. Without them we can only survive or at best maintain ourselves at existing levels.

Making space is a key activity for people in the Learning Company. Giving yourself, and others, headroom, is crucial to development. Getting the amount of space right is critical: too little and we feel cramped, claustrophobic; too much and we feel insecure, agoraphobic. This applies to physical, social and mental space.

Here are some ideas for creating space in the Learning Company – as a manager, facilitator, counsellor, chairperson, project leader:

- stop talking and listen actively instead
- don't always respond to requests for expert advice when expected
- allow and encourage small silences
- avoid teaching
- slow things down – people, discussions, processes
- question the relevance of tasks
- encourage reflection and deepen discussions
- sit within the group, not at the front
- leave the group to work, on their own
- build on people's comments, make linkages, offer options
- look for normal practices and reverse them.

In the world of work most of us are better at filling things up with 'busyness' than we are at emptying and opening up space, but it is important that we make a conscious effort to do so.

FOLLOW-UP READING

Kemp, N., 'Self-development: Practical Issues for Facilitators', *Journal of European Industrial Training*, 13(5), pages 1–28 (1989).

Glimpse 22
Measuring the quality of your learning climate

One of the defining characteristics of the Learning Company is of being a place that encourages everyone who works in it or who has contact with it to learn. It has the 'learning habit' so that actions taken for reasons of production, marketing, problem solving or customer service also yield a harvest of reflections, insights and new ideas for action.

Here is a simple questionnaire that you can use to measure the learning climate of your company, department or team.

Learning climate questionnaire

For each of the following ten dimensions, ring the number that you think best represents the quality of the Learning Climate in your company, 1 being very poor, 7 being excellent:

1. Physical environment
The amount and quality of space and privacy afforded to people; the temperature, noise, ventilation and comfort levels.

People are cramped with little privacy and poor conditions	1 2 3 4 5 6 7	People have plenty of space, privacy and good surroundings

2. Learning resources
Numbers, quality and availability of training and development staff, also books, films, training packages, equipment, etc.

Very few or no trained people, poor resources and equipment	1 2 3 4 5 6 7	Many development people and lots of resources; very good facilities

3. Encouragement to learn

The extent to which people feel encouraged to have ideas, take risks, experiment and learn new ways of doing old tasks.

| Little encouragement to learn; there are low expectations of people in terms of new skills and abilities | 1 2 3 4 5 6 7 | People are encouraged to learn at all times and to extend themselves and their knowledge |

4. Communications

How open and free is the flow of information? Do people express ideas and opinions easily and openly?

| Feelings kept to self; secretive; information is hoarded | 1 2 3 4 5 6 7 | People are usually ready to give their views and pass on information |

5. Rewards

How well rewarded are people for effort? Is recognition given for good work or are people punished and blamed?

| People are ignored but then blamed when things go wrong | 1 2 3 4 5 6 7 | People are recognized for good work and rewarded for effort and learning |

6. Conformity

The extent to which people are expected to conform to rules, norms, regulations, policies rather than think for themselves.

| There is conformity to rules and standards at all times – no personal responsibility taken or given | 1 2 3 4 5 6 7 | People manage themselves and do their work as they see fit; great emphasis on taking personal responsibility |

7. Value placed on ideas

How much are ideas, opinions and suggestions sought out, encouraged and valued?

| People are 'not paid to think'; their ideas are not valued | 1 2 3 4 5 6 7 | Efforts are made to get people to put ideas forward; there is a view that the future rests on people's ideas |

8. Practical help available

The extent to which people help each other, lend a hand, offer skills, knowledge or support.

People don't help
each other; there is
unwillingness to pool
or share resources

1 2 3 4 5 6 7

People very willing and
helpful; pleasure is
taken in the success of
others

9. Warmth and support

How friendly are people in the company? Do people support, trust and like one another?

Little warmth and
support; this is a
cold, isolating place

1 2 3 4 5 6 7

Warm and friendly place;
people enjoy coming to
work; good relationships
= good work

10. Standards

The emphasis placed upon quality in all things; people set challenging standards for themselves and each other.

Low standards and
quality; no one really
gives a damn

1 2 3 4 5 6 7

High standards;
everyone cares and people
pick each other up on
work quality

Scoring

If your score comes to 30 or less, you're working in a *poor* learning climate. Learning Companies aspire to scores in the 50 to 70 range as the best guarantee of future survival, maintenance and development.

If you carry out a survey of the company, you may find differences in the various parts of the organization. How do you explain this? The person in charge of a department usually has the biggest influence on the learning climate. Does that person have the development of an excellent learning climate as a key objective?

REFERENCE

This learning climate questionnaire is adapted from M. J. Pedler and T. H. Boydell's book *Managing Yourself*, Fontana (1985) and Gower Press (1990).

A Learning Company has a healthy climate fit for human beings to live and learn in. Many companies today are less than healthy, and some are downright toxic. That is to say they are 'poisonous'. You can take a climate check on your company with the Organizational Toxicity Index below.

For each of the following ten questions choose one of the responses – a, b or c – on the basis of which is truest, in *your* experience, most of the time.

Organizational Toxicity Index

'In my company . . .

1. sexist and racist remarks are commonplace and tolerated by management.'

a This is not a problem.   ☐
b This is something of a problem.   ☐
c This is a big problem for me and others. ☐

2. praise is much rarer than criticism.'

a This is not a problem.   ☐
b This is something of a problem.   ☐
c This is a big problem for me and others. ☐

3. you get little information about your own performance.'

a This is not a problem.   ☐
b This is something of a problem.   ☐
c This is a big problem for me and others. ☐

4. there is competitive pressure from fellow employees to work long hours.'

a This is not a problem.   ☐
b This is something of a problem.   ☐
c This is a big problem for me and others. ☐

5. there is little concern shown for members' health and welfare.'

a This is not a problem.   ☐
b This is something of a problem.   ☐
c This is a big problem for me and others. ☐

6. making admissions of mistakes or failures is "career limiting".'

a This is not a problem.   ☐
b This is something of a problem.   ☐
c This is a big problem for me and others.   ☐

7. all management decisions are justified in terms of the "bottom line", that is, solely on financial grounds.'

a This is not a problem.   ☐
b This is something of a problem.   ☐
c This is a big problem for me and others.   ☐

8. there are a lot of hierarchical distinctions made in terms of conditions, perks like cars and offices, canteens and so on.'

a This is not a problem.   ☐
b This is something of a problem.   ☐
c This is a big problem for me and others.   ☐

9. there is little diversity in management – most are male, white, etc.'

a This is not a problem.   ☐
b This is something of a problem.   ☐
c This is a big problem for me and others.   ☐

10. it's very hard to get people to listen to you and your ideas.'

a This is not a problem.   ☐
b This is something of a problem.   ☐
c This is a big problem for me and others.   ☐

Scoring

Score 0 for every a, 1 for every b and 2 for every c. The minimum score is 0, the maximum 20. If you scored less than 5, then your company is comparatively healthy, although there may be some points that need attention. If you scored 6 to 12, then your company is quite toxic – to the point that many people's performance must be impaired. If you score more than 12, your company is getting to the point where it is not fit for human beings to live and work in. Time to do the decent thing?

FOLLOW-UP READING

A comprehensive version of the OTI questionnaire is available from the authors at The Learning Company Project at the address given on page 213.

One of the characteristics of a Learning Company is that many of the members have acquired and value training and development skills. We heard a few years ago of a Bonn department store where 73 out of 450 employees are professionally qualified trainers (Holland 1986). That is almost one in seven people – how does *your* company stand up to that standard?

It is not just a question of how many of us have professional qualifications, although that would be a useful start, but of how seriously we take the issue of creating development opportunities and the excellent learning climate which ensures that everyone acquires and keeps the learning habit. This is one of the building blocks of the Learning Company and one that we know how to do, so there is little excuse for neglecting it.

For all developers and trainers there is always the question of what is the right, the most appropriate style for this type of skill, for this particular person, under these conditions? David Megginson has provided a useful summary of three styles together with a questionnaire to help you diagnose your own preferred style and to clarify the alternatives.

Questionnaire

For each statement, circle the number that best represents your usual style in helping people to learn things.

1. 'Before telling people about a job I want them to do, I work out, stage by stage, what's involved in it.'
Seldom   0   1   2   3   4   5   6   Often

2. 'I actively seek out opportunities for people to develop themselves through doing new things at work.'
Seldom   0   1   2   3   4   5   6   Often

3. 'I listen to people's ideas and help them fit these into their broad plans for work and life.'
Seldom   0   1   2   3   4   5   6   Often

4. 'When I have something I want people to do, I give them very clear instructions.'
Seldom   0   1   2   3   4   5   6   Often

5. 'When helping people to learn, I help them plan how to meet challenges at work.'
Seldom   0   1   2   3   4   5   6   Often

6. 'I ask people questions that help them think through why they want to do things.'
Seldom   0   1   2   3   4   5   6   Often

7. 'I check that people have understood their instructions clearly.'
Seldom   0   1   2   3   4   5   6   Often

8. 'I am prepared to let people try new things, even if there is a risk that they may not do the job well.'
Seldom   0   1   2   3   4   5   6   Often

9. 'I am interested in what people do outside work and how this fits in or conflicts with work activities.'
Seldom   0   1   2   3   4   5   6   Often

10. 'I check up on things I've asked people to do, and let them know how they did.'
Seldom   0   1   2   3   4   5   6   Often

11. 'I encourage people to review how they perform and plan how to improve.'
Seldom   0   1   2   3   4   5   6   Often

12. 'I sit down with people and help them think through where they are going in their career.'
Seldom   0   1   2   3   4   5   6   Often

Scoring

To calculate your scores, total up the numbers for each of the questions in three columns as follows:

Instructor		Coach		Mentor	
Q1	☐	Q2	☐	Q3	☐
Q4	☐	Q5	☐	Q6	☐
Q7	☐	Q8	☐	Q9	☐
Q10	☐	Q11	☐	Q12	☐
Totals —		—		—	

The higher your score in any one column, the more you tend to that style of helping others to learn.

Interpreting your score

Well, is your style good or bad? First, you can ask a colleague to complete the questionnaire and compare your scoring with your colleagues. Best of all, you could ask the people who you are trying to help learn. A score of 15 or more for any of these shows quite a strong preference, while 5 or less would show a marked avoidance. If you have pursued a 'central tendency' on the questionnaire, your scores will average around 12 to 16. Why not do the questionnaire again now, and use the whole range of marks – let's say you can't use the 2, 3 and 4 more than twice each.

Dimension	Instructor	Coach	Mentor
Focus of help	Task	Results of job	Development of person throughout life
Timespan	A day or two	A month to a year	Career or lifetime
Approach to helping	'Show and tell' – give supervised practise	Explore problem together and set up opportunities to try out new skills	Act as friend willing to play 'devil's advocate', listen and question to enlarge awareness
Associated activities	Analysing task; clear instruction; supervise practise; give feedback on results at once	Jointly identify the problem; create development opportunity and review	Link work with other parts of life; clarify broad and long-term aims and purpose in life
Ownership	Helper	Shared	Learner
Attitude to ambiguity	Eliminate	Use it as a challenge – as a puzzle to be solved	Accept as being part of the exciting world
Benefits to the company	Standard, accurate performance	Goal-directed performance oriented to improving and being creative	Conscious questioning approach to the mission of the company

Table G24.1 Three ways of helping people to learn

Table G24.1 describes the styles. This should help you to locate yourself more accurately and perhaps give you some ideas for things you might do differently or try out next time you are helping someone to learn.

REFERENCE AND FOLLOW-UP READING

Holland, G. 'Excellence in Industry', speech to Institute of Directors at the Dorchester Hotel, London (11 February 1986).

Megginson, D. F. and M. J. Pedler, *Self-development: A Facilitator's Guide*, McGraw-Hill (forthcoming).

Striving to 'delight' our customers

One of the basic ideas behind Total Quality Management (TQM) is that of striving to 'delight' our customers – internal and external. This is important for the Learning Company, not only because, like any other it needs good customers, but because it does much of its work through high-quality relationships with others.

This activity will not only help you improve things with your customers, it will also help you build up valuable skills in creating and improving good relationships. Rosabeth Kantor has called this 'becoming PALS – Pooling, Allying and Linking across Companies', which she sees as central to the new way of doing business.

This activity has seven steps and a map to help you delight your customers. It takes time and involves taking a risk with at least one of your existing customers, so you need to think carefully about it before making a start.

Step 1: Who are our customers?
- Identify your main customers, naming them as specifically as possible.
- Choose six of these and write their names in segments of the first ring of the customer map, given in Figure G25.1.

Step 2: What will delight them?
- For each customer ask yourself, 'What do they want from me?' and 'What will delight them?'
- Write your perceptions for each customer in the segments of the second ring on the map.

Step 3: How well are we doing?
- Estimate how well you think you are doing regarding each of the things that you think will delight your customers and put this in the third ring.
- Try to make this measurable, e.g., 'we are taking 20 days to turn around our orders', or with a simple scale, from 'doing rather badly' through to 'doing very well', even 'exceeding customer expectations'.

Step 4: How can our customers help us to do better?
- Although they are often 'always right', as a supplier you have needs and rights, too.
- To delight the customer you need a partnership that works well for both.

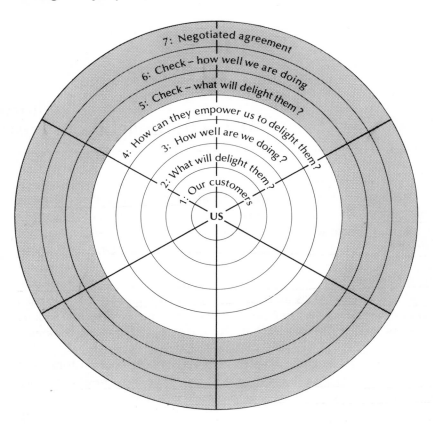

Figure G25.1 A customer map

- Work through the following three questions, perhaps using your colleagues to help you brainstorm responses:
  - What do your customers do already that helps you (and that you would therefore like them to continue to do or to do even more of)?
  - What do they do that makes it harder for you to delight them (and that you would like them to do less of, indeed, stop altogether if possible)?
  - What don't they do that would help you delight them (and that you would like them to start doing)?
Enter these into the fourth ring on the diagram.

Step 5: Checking out what will delight your customers
- From now on the diagram rings are shaded – this means that you can only do these in partnership with your customers.
- Arrange a meeting with one of your customers, explaining carefully why you want the meeting, namely, to explore how you could improve your service to them. You could use the format from Step 4 above but asking the questions from their perspective, e.g., 'What is it that you do that delights them and that they would like you to continue and do more of?, etc.

• Check the responses out with your own assessment from Step 2. At this point just *listen*; don't get into discussion or negotiation, let alone argument.

Step 6: Checking out how well we are doing at delighting our customers
• Check out your earlier judgements at Step 3 with the new data from Step 5.

Step 7: Negotiating an agreement
• If the customer agrees, you can negotiate a new contract to cover the following:
  • *aims* what you will do/will not do to delight them
  • *support* what they will do/will not do to help you in these
  • *review* the programme you will follow for monitoring and review. It goes without saying that this negotiating must be carried out in a win:win spirit. The aim is to improve an existing relationship that might be good but could be better.

Learning companies develop exceptional skills in negotiating partnerships with the 'key players' in their orbit. Facilitating networks of production and supply is one of the things they do best.

REFERENCE

Kantor, R. M., *When Giants Learn to Dance*, Unwin Hyman (1990).

Glimpse 26
Management development policy in the Learning Company

Companies are managed by people who are living their careers. What happens to people in their career paths has a major impact on the company. There are two aspects to careers – the *structural*, that is, the sequence of jobs or tasks, and the *developmental*, which is what people learn and how they change during their careers.

Management development is that which is done deliberately to manage these two aspects of peoples' careers. The tactics of management development include structural interventions, such as succession planning, career appraisal, career structuring, and developmental interventions, courses, provision of open learning materials and mentoring arrangements. However, unless these individual-level tactics contribute to, and form part of, corporate policy they will only be locally or remedially useful. Management development policy is concerned with the coordination of corporate policy with structural and developmental management development interventions.

From this viewpoint, a six-level model of management development policy can be identified. Only companies operating at the fifth or sixth levels are likely to be able to function as Learning Companies.

- At level one there is essentially no planned management development. People develop to some extent, of course, as a result of living and working, but this is natural or by chance. According to recent surveys, half of UK companies are at this level. Only very small and dynamic companies are likely to have people who develop to make their best contribution under these circumstances.
- At level two there are isolated and piecemeal structural or developmental tactics, probably to meet some crisis such as a skills shortage, a succession problem or a failure in business performance due to a lack of collective competence such as low financial awareness or customer care. When people are given development opportunities or career planning at this level they usually bear no relation to one another.
- At level three, structural and developmental tactics are coordinated. Development needs identified at appraisals are followed up and career plans take potential into account and incorporate planned development to realize it. A

formal paperwork system exists. The snag here is that companies do not stay the same for long. When changes come as a result of policy initiatives or crises, the well-laid management development plans are obsolete.

- At level four, management development policy and planning is closely linked to corporate planning. This includes what is known and planned and also what is uncertain and what the main contingencies are. Management development practice is based on judgements about what will stay the same and what will change or is uncertain about future jobs, roles and tasks.

- The fifth level includes the processes we saw at levels two to four, but now has an input to corporate policy formation. Data on the company's collective competence, creative visions of possible alternative futures arising from career planning or development workshops using key policy issues as live case material contribute to the policy debate. Human resource directors make a critical input to the company's strategic opportunities based on their reading of the cumulative abilities, potentials and vision of staff alongside their marketing, technical and financial colleagues.

- At the sixth level, a management development perspective not only makes inputs to corporate policy, but also illuminates the policy-forming process. Previous policy and its implementation is reviewed, critiqued and learned from; new directions are chosen with exploratory or experimental objectives in mind; new ventures have built in monitoring and evaluation mechanisms. When the company takes a risk, it does everything it can to maximize the learning from that initiative, whatever the business outcome.

This six-step ladder offers a possible agenda for the people development function and a way of making a contribution to becoming a Learning Company. The ladder can be used to take stock of where you are now (in our experience, people in the human resource function always believe they are higher on the ladder than do people in the operating arms of the company). This sort of debate can be useful in checking how well the company is doing in terms of creating opportunities for people to participate in policy making and to see their career futures in the corporate context.

FOLLOW-UP READING

Burgoyne, J. G., 'Management Development for the Individual *and* the Organization', *Personnel Management*, pages 40–44 (June 1988).

Glimpse 27
Collaborative career planning

Ed Schein has described careers as the result of a series of deals struck between individuals and the organizations they work for. It follows that the productivity of careers – for people and their companies – depends on how well informed each party is about the other's needs and intentions and also on the quality of the negotiating process. Many personnel problems are the result of bad deals between individuals and companies.

Collaborative career planning creates good deals for both parties. While the specifics of these vary with culture and circumstances, the general features of this process are that:

- individuals regularly take stock of themselves in terms of
  - what they're good at
  - what they have the potential to be good at
  - what abilities they are using and not using now
  - what they want to do and fulfil in the future
  - what is their image of their career
  - their view of the company's future and of particular developments to which they could contribute
  - avenues for personal development that might serve the company's interest as well as their own
- people have the opportunity to talk through their thoughts with those responsible for negotiating their careers on behalf of the company so that they have knowledge of and are involved in
  - company policy issues, options and likely areas of change and development
  - the implications of these for structures, roles, needed competencies and abilities in the future
  - a view of the opportunities and constraints that this will create in terms of career possibilities
- these discussions provide for an exchange of information allowing for mutual adjustment of views and, as part of a regular process of taking stock and discussing possibilities, they create a better informed background for making decisions, both at the personal and corporate levels.

Collaborative career planning can be more or less formal or systematized. It can be integrated with other processes such as appraisal, performance review and business planning. Information from career discussion can be fed into central databases to create a view of the collective competence and aspirations of staff who, in turn, are better informed about what they should choose and negotiate for themselves.

REFERENCE AND FOLLOW-UP READING

Schein, E., *Career Dynamics*, Addison-Wesley (1978).

Germaine, C. and J. G. Burgoyne, 'Self-development and Career Planning: An Exercise in Mutual Benefit', *Personnel Management* (April 1984).

Glimpse 28
Finding good form

Prematurely abandoning new organizational forms before developing the new desired habits and actions is a common fault among would-be change makers – as we see in Glimpse 65. Choosing a good form for your unit, department or company can be a tricky one. What is the right structure?

Here are but four of the possibilities in a continuum from hierarchy – the enduring and most mechanistic form – through matrix and cloverleaf, to network – the most nebulous and organic form. While going through these, ask yourself 'Where is my company (or unit) on this continuum?' and 'What would be the best form(s) for my company?'

• *Hierarchy*

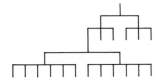

The classical, bureaucratic form promising order, control, predictability. Works best in stable conditions and is slow to change. All know their place and tend to be punished, or at least not rewarded, for innovating, taking risks or asking questions. Claims about the end of hierarchy are probably premature given that, on some reckonings, it has been around for 2000 years. This form, however, has some serious limitations for companies that need to adapt and flex quickly.

• *Matrix*

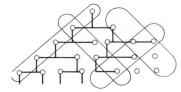

This is where a hierarchy remains but is overlain by project teams and groupings as a response to novel demands and problems. A matrix often has functional departments – marketing, production, R & D, etc. – with product, brand or business area teams cutting across the vertical lines. In theory, the matrix gives strong alignment *and* task forces, which enables the company to draw widely on available functional skills and knowledge. A problem is that hierarchy tends to reassert itself, especially around 'crunch' resource issues such as budgets, members' careers or big risks. Some form of matrix is probably an operating necessity in most modern companies. An individual's ability to balance their several roles is a key skill.

- *Cloverleaf*

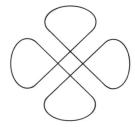

This form has done away with hierarchy – almost! Here there's a small, core team managing the radiating, often-changing work teams and functions. Often only the core are full-time or long service. Work groups may contain a lot of part-timers, self-employed or short-term contractors. Cloverleafs deal well with rapidly changing circumstances and short-life tasks. Highly skilled and professional workers may demand the sort of autonomy and variety of contracts that they offer. Companies may find it hard to operate in fashion markets without parts or the whole structured in this way.

- *Networks*

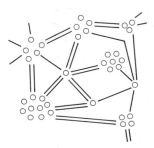

These are much more loosely coupled systems of people and groups that work together. Here there is no hierarchy or centre but more 'heterarchy' based on job leadership by the best-equipped group or the person who originates the project. People are in business and can be mobilized at a number of levels – as self-employed units, members of small firms and as part of the whole network. It is much harder to say where the network company starts and finishes; each member, group or node has many links inside and outside.

There is no ideal form for the Learning Company. Perhaps it is in the fortunate position of having a greater repertoire of forms that it can use or transform itself into – in whole or in part – as best fitted for certain markets, products or people's wishes. Have you got the right forms in place? Have you a rich enough repertoire? Can you move from this into that form when it's appropriate or does change of form only come with each sweep of the new broom?

FOLLOW-UP READING

Here are three writers who address the theme of form:

Mintzberg, H., *Mintzberg on Management*, Free Press (1989).

Handy, C., *The Age of Unreason*, Basic Books (1989).

Lievegoed, B. C. G., *The Developing Organization*, Celestial Arts (1973), Blackwell (1990, rev ed.).

Glimpse 29
Special competencies for the Learning Company

Organizations often attempt to define the competencies that are needed in certain jobs or for certain career paths. These tend to be oriented to the skills that are needed to allow the organization to continue to do what it is already doing well. This is a necessary and useful process, but taken alone as a major component of a human resource development strategy it will tend to fix or reinforce current or historical ways of doing things in a company.

There seem to be two ways out of this problem: recognizing learning as a competence and recognizing forecasting as a competence.

In our work on self-development we suggest that the skills of learning itself are creativity, mental agility and balanced learning habits and suggest various ways of developing these. Developing learning competence in itself is an attractive option in the Learning Company because it offers the prospect of people becoming more flexible in their ability to take on and master quickly new tasks.

Gareth Morgan offers another option: developing the skills of forecasting. He suggests that the skills of reading the future are themselves a crucial area of managerial competence. He particularly uses the notion of spotting 'fracture lines' – the emerging major discontinuities in the social and economic system of which any company is embedded, the reaction to which will significantly determine the company's future. Such changes are easy to identify in retrospect – an oil crisis, ecological crisis, major changes in political power, privatization – but what will future fracture lines be.

REFERENCES

Pedler, M., J. Burgoyne and T. Boydell, *A Manager's Guide to Self-Development*, McGraw-Hill (1986).

Morgan, G., *Riding the Waves of Change*, Jossey Bass (1988).

Glimpse 30
Creating organizations fit for the human spirit

Much of the work that architects do in the renovation and conversion of old buildings is concerned with making space. They create large, open areas inside, removing dividing walls and even parts of floors, letting in light through larger windows, softening the inside/outside boundary further by bringing in lots of greenery and so on.

> Architecture means the thoughtful housing of the human spirit in the physical world.
> (William Meyer, *Contemporary Architects*)

At the present time, the prime task is to clear space in over-supervised, over-regulated regions of our working world in order to encourage more rather than fewer organization members to boldly go where they have not gone before. Space making – gaps, breaks, openings, windows, elbow room, and so on – is also opportunity making. Space making as a managerial task is a striking reversal of the bureaucrat's concern with space filling via job descriptions, key results areas, departmental boundaries, organization charts and so on.

Space making, however, is not simple or straightforward; it is not a task for modern Cromwells laying waste with ball and chain. Some of the old walls and floors need to remain – space in the unbounded sense of a void, abyss, waste, infinity, is not likely to offer opportunities to us who have been brought up inside the confines of the bureaucratic form. Too much space and we will lose our sense of ourselves, lose our identities, and not be able to learn. Appropriate space or opportunity making is a sensitive and constructive act requiring artistry that must operate, ultimately, at the level of the individual.

Despite the individualistic nature of these challenges, there are some generalizations we can make, some architectural devices that are becoming common in space making in organizations. Here are some examples from physcial architecture with their possible organizational interpretation(s):

- removal of dividing walls
- partial removal of floors
- outside staircases; putting service pipes, etc. outside

- demolish departmental boundaries
- removing levels of supervision
- hiving off service functions

- central courtyards, wells, atriums

- add balconies
- re-cycling old bricks, etc.

- use historical objects as sculpture
- lots of inside greenery

- put skylights in the roof

- put in bigger windows
- preserve historical objects

- decentralize functions, remove central services
- encourage outside trading
- re-train people, encourage radical job changes
- celebrate differences, encourage expression
- blur home/work/community boundaries
- open up top management processes for inspection and comment
- encourage secondments outside
- bring back selected retirees as part-time help – and not just top people.

Glimpse 31
Autopoesis

Traditionally, theories about organizations have depicted change as something that comes from without, from the environment. The 'environment' has often been seen as something unfriendly, dangerous or 'hypercompetitive', to quote a modern favourite. Two Chilean scientists, Humberto Maturana and Francisco Varela, have recently challenged this taken-for-granted view. They argue that organizations are not 'open systems' interacting with the 'environment', but are closed, autonomous systems of interactions, making reference only to themselves. They go on to say that this autonomy, circularity and self-reference allows living systems to self-renew or self-produce. According to this view, the organization and identity of the company is its most important product. They have coined the word 'autopoesis' for this capacity for self-production.

An autopoetic standpoint on the company turns the world upside down. Instead of seeing the company as at the mercy of its environment, the environment is seen as a reflection of and as part of the organization. Thus, a company produces itself and its own 'environment' as part of that production. The 'environment' is a part of its inner indentity.

This is hard to see at first. It's a bit like one of those figure/ground conundrums – the old lady/young girl or vase/candlestick – you look and look, but you can't see it and, then suddenly, there it is! Here is an example that might help.

G & G Fans was a small engineering concern with 20 employees selling over 70 per cent of its output to an air-conditioning company. When its main customer was taken over by a French business, who had their own supplier of fans, G & G faced extinction – unless they could find new customers quickly.

On the day their new marketing consultant arrived, she noticed that the neat little factory was almost half full of packed fans ready for delivery. However, what surprised her was that Barney, the owner, in his blue overalls, was over in the corner excitedly discussing a new prototype fan on wheels for garage fume extraction, with most of the workforce clustered round him. 'Who's responsible for sales?', she asked. 'Well, I do the invoices, like', came the reply.

On being told by the consultant that she would only work with him if he went on to marketing full-time, Barney refused point blank, saying, 'I'm an engineer, you see, I make things, invent things. I can't sell, that's a job for folks like you with smart suits and silver tongues'. Further discussion revealed that Barney and his people never went outside the factory if they could help it, they always got customers to come to them, they were unsure of themselves off their own patch and saw the world outside as vast and scary. They wanted the consultant to find them a new customer so they could get back to their fan on wheels.

It is very clear in this little firm that the people 'produce' their own organization and its 'environment' every day. Their picture of the world outside the factory and their experience of life inside are part of the same whole. The consultant can start at either end, but if the firm is to survive, both inside *and* outside perceptions and actions have to change.

Of course, this 'production' of inside and outside worlds is not just a small-company phenomenon. When you see managers in large concerns talking up the 'opposition', the 'global marketplace', the need to 'fight for survival', etc., etc., the same process is being enacted. Whereas Barney didn't want to lift his eyes to the window to see what was going on out there, these managers 'know' only too well what it's like out there in that jungle – it's so tough that you'd never think of approaching 'competitors' to see what you could learn, to open up a new market together, to pool resources to develop a much-needed new product.

FOLLOW-UP READING

Morgan, G., *Images of Organization*, Sage Publications (1986) gives a good account of autopoesis in his Chapter 8. References to Maturana and Varela's papers are given in his bibliography.

Glimpse 32
Transforming the company

Unlike problem solving or trouble shooting, organizational transformation means that everyone changes the way they do things – individually and as a whole company. Transformation always poses the questions 'Why am I here?' and 'Why are we in business?', 'What is my *purpose*?' and 'What is *our* purpose together?'

These are questions about fundamental purpose and the process of asking them is likely to be unsettling, exciting, disturbing, energizing and disruptive. If these questions are *really* asked in a company, they are unlikely to be answered by superficial changes of the 'redesign the logos and the letterheads' variety.

Transformation in individuals and companies requires space, time and proper support. It does not happen overnight, nor without the necessary thinking through before, during and after, nor without the necessary skills of supporting, challenging and developing. Here is an example of transformation in practice.

Billiton, a Shell subsidiary and an international metals company with a turnover of $1.5bn had accumulated losses of $750m and was being considered for disposal by its multi-national parent. A new CEO decided that one last chance was possible. He ordered a rigorous analysis of 'the businesses we are in and why we are in them'. Product divisions were replaced by 'core businesses' and power was developed from head office to operating companies. Head office would lose half its establishment and change its role from 'command centre' to 'service provider' to the operating companies and 'monitor/auditor' for the shareholders.

Top-down prescription of the detailed way of working in head office was resisted and left to emerge from a planned consultation process. Over 18 months this programme included:

- attitude surveys of all 250 head office staff at six-month intervals (the first showed that people saw themselves in a tense and stressful situation)
- departmental work groups set up after the first survey to consider local needs and whole company issues – initially this took 30 per cent of staff time
- a multi-disciplinary task force to coordinate the work groups and the management team, supported by consultants

- specific consultancy skills were deployed to individuals and departments who asked for them; a full advisory and counselling service was offered to those who were to leave or who might opt to do so
- the second and third surveys gave progress reports, identifying positive changes and continuing concerns; training, team-building and other resource inputs were based on this data.

The results for the business were good: return on capital went from 2 per cent to 17 per cent over two years and the second year showed a profit after tax of $262m. For individuals it had often been traumatic, although group and team work meant difficulties could be shared. The managing team, who had remained throughout, felt they had changed significantly – personally and in the way they did business together.

Nietzsche's dramatic, 'that which does not kill me makes me strong' is worth pondering for those contemplating transformation – personally or organizationally. It cannot be done without upheaval on such a scale that we will all require support and help to come through it. When and if we come through, however, we will be strengthened, fitter and perhaps wiser.

FOLLOW-UP READING

Benjamin, G., and C. Mabey, 'Organizational Transformation and the Self', *Management Education & Development*, 21(5) pages 327–334 (1990).

Glimpse 33
Stars to steer by

Since ancient times people have dreamed of better futures. Often these visions have served as stars to steer by when things are difficult or uncertain. Now, as our previous over-reliance upon scientific thinking is ebbing, we are turning to some of the ancient mysteries in order to rediscover the art of leadership to add to the principles of management.

At some stage, of course, vision has to be tested against reality, but not now. A dose of 'healthy reality' administered too soon will kill off the most promising shoots of imagination. Without an image of the future we have no good reason for changing what we do now. Why change or learn when we have nowhere we want to go? Those of us who pride ourselves on our scepticism and 'realism' (many of us protecting our precious and deeply buried idealism) have an important role to play – somewhere along the line from vision to action – but not now.

You don't have to be Moses to day-dream the 'promised land'. Any company that wants to be a Learning Company must find a way, first, of collectively dreaming up a picture of what this looks like for them for, as we have said often in this book, there are no blueprints. What follows is a way of working with a group of others to generate a vision of your idea of the Learning Company.

First of all, we define vision as your hope for and belief in a desired future. To do this requires the ability to rise above your current, everyday reality in order to dream up a picture of how things *could* be and how you would *like* them to be. Your picture of the Learning Company comes from many sources and Figure G33.1 shows a selection of them.

Start working on these questions by dividing into pairs or threes and ask yourselves these and any other questions you can think of that relate to the future Learning Company. Record the responses. It can help if you encourage people to be very specific, asking them, for example, 'What do our new customers wear?', 'What colour is the new office?', 'What does the place sound like?', 'What do we do outside work?' and so on. (To get more ideas, look at Glimpse 5.)

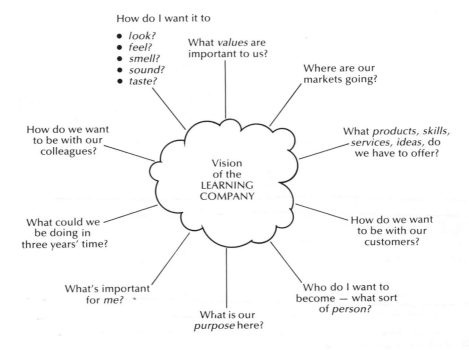

How do I want it to
- *look?*
- *feel?*
- *smell?*
- *sound?*
- *taste?*

What *values* are important to us?

Where are our markets going?

How do we want to be with our colleagues?

What *products, skills, services, ideas,* do we have to offer?

Vision of the LEARNING COMPANY

What could we be doing in three years' time?

How do we want to be with our customers?

What's important for *me?*

Who do I want to become — what sort of *person?*

What is our *purpose* here?

Figure G33.1 The elements forming our vision of the Learning Company

Next, find a way of presenting your findings back to the whole group. Do think about some of the less obvious ways of doing it. A poster can be very effective, as can someone telling a short story about how the old company turned into the new. A job advertisement for the new company would give a strong flavour, while the dramatically inclined might choose to offer a poem, a play or a mime to get the message over. Why not use video if you have it?

Whatever you do, find a way of getting people to listen, watch, see in the right way – turn the lights off while you talk, hang your posters like a picture gallery and walk people round or give a speech outside.

The next stage is to create something out of the whole group. Again there are various ways of doing this. Which pictures or messages were particularly exciting? Which directions look most promising? Which presentations did people enthuse about?

Select one or more ideas to do some further work on and form into teams around these ideas (perhaps this would be a good time to have a social break to reintegrate the whole and allow for people to give up their individual ownership of ideas to the whole group).

Each team could then work together to create symbols, images or designs to embody the picture or a key aspect of it. There will be concrete ways of doing this, some of which may suit your particular organization. For example, people have made badges, coats of arms, T-shirts, logos, mock-ups of shop fronts, vehicle paint designs, brochures or letterheads.

It is important to make time to let people get on with this creative work. Most of us, especially in the company of a few colleagues, have more creative and artistic potential than we ever use. Being creative – in concrete form – is a key aspect of creating stars to steer by.

Exhibit the finished works and have an appropriate celebration. What comes next depends on your situation, whether it be commissioning a team to act on a chosen vision or publishing the exhibits to a wider audience. What's the next step?

Glimpse 34
Learning Company values

Rather as you'd find in the 'excellent' company or the 'quality' company, values are at the centre of the Learning Company. Because of the need to adapt and change intelligently and to be consciously developing as a whole organism, the Learning Company does not put its faith in enduring structures and processes but sees these as temporary. Values are more enduring and though changing over time do so rather more slowly. One of the key tasks for the Learning Company is to try and embrace the values of all its members, who all wish to be valued.

This is an endless task for who is to say, ultimately, who the members of a Learning Company are. However, a useful start can be made with this simple activity that can be done with small and large groups of people, although larger groups will require a more sophisticated data gathering and analysis process than that described here.

- Begin by suggesting that a certain agreed set of values are central to the idea of the Learning Company and that the purpose of this activity is to determine what these values might be for this company.
- In pairs or small groups, members answer the question 'What values would a Learning Company hold to be of central importance?' Each person should take a little time to think for themselves first before discussing their list.
- Lists are taken from pairs or small groups and collated centrally. A flipchart will suffice for a smallish number of people. For larger groups or whole companies, polling and computer analysis may be useful. As an example, here is a recent list from a group of 23 people:

experimentation	feedback
learning	equality
participation	collaboration
creativity	contingency
feminine	win:win
differences	freedom
development	listening
self-control	celebration
self-management	self-denial.
information	

- How are these values displayed in what we do: in our mission statement, in the way we manage, in the way we treat customers and so on?

The information generated from this activity can be used to review all aspects of company functioning as well as providing the most solid ground available for deciding what structures and procedures to establish.

Glimpse 35
Working with diversity

Diversity is one of the most vital aspects of the Learning Company. How a company manages to work with the diversity it has is one of the keys to learning and productivity. For many years companies have tried to suppress diversity, preferring sameness and uniformity because this is easier to manage. Acknowledging diversity or differences can lead to loss of control, which is something we always fear when we are in charge of something.

How can we not only recognize and acknowledge diversity, but positively use the differences between us to create power in the Learning Company? The whole cannot be enhanced without first splitting; division is needed before greater synthesis and synergy can be brought about; learning begins in difference – between me and you, between what I expected and what happened, between what is and what could be.

We all need practice in working with the potentially explosive diversity of ourselves. While suppressing differences is one way of avoiding an explosion, it is not the learning way. Learning Companies have to create within themselves a vessel strong enough to survive the occasional explosion so that learning, not just to acknowledge, but to celebrate and capitalize on diversity, can take place.

Here is a simple but powerful activity for a group of people of any size that will need skilled facilitation.

- Elicit from a group of people the key differences that they see among them. List these. Obvious examples might be:

women and men	engineering and others
over 40 and under 40	administrative and others
Asian and white	managers and others.
part-time and full-time workers	

- Choose a dimension of difference and ask the group concerned to split along these lines and stand in a different part of the room. (This activity can also be done remotely with a whole company by questionnaire and feedback means if a state of readiness exists – rather like postal chess.) In each of the two groups, separate into pairs. In each of the pairs complete these three sentences with your partner:

- What's important to me about being a _____ , is ....
- As a _____ I bring to this company ....
- The extent to which this company empowers me to live out and make use of my potential as a _____ is ....
- When each person has completed these in their pair, form a plenary session in each of the two groups and summarize the responses to the three sentences as briefly but as fully as possible.
- In the middle of the room, each group reads out its collective responses to the other, who listen in silence.
- Now split along another difference and repeat the last three steps as before. Continue until three or four major aspects of diversity have been explored.

This can be a powerful and rewarding activity. It is also capable of being adapted in various ways, including the whole company vision suggested above. You will need to judge for yourself what level of diversity and difference your company is ready to deal with and, indeed, whether this potent avenue of learning and development is open or whether you have to keep the lid firmly on at this time. There is a spectrum of developmental responses to diversity that starts with recognition (in many companies differences between the way, say, men and women are treated simply go unnoticed, they are invisible to most) and moves through acceptance to valuing this difference:

Spectrum of developmental responses to diversity

0	1	2	3	4	5
Unnoticed	Recognize	Become aware	Tolerate/ accept	Respect	Value

Glimpse 36
Personal development plans (PDPs)

Personal development plans (PDPs) are part of the 'software' of the Learning Company – each person should have one in some form. In some companies, learning and development is such a part of the natural order of things that these plans are agreements between individuals with no central recording, while other big companies that have adopted the idea, have attached it to performance review and produced rather too much paperwork.

The idea is simple. Each of us is in a process of development as person and worker. We can become aware of this process and, to some extent, direct ourselves towards desired ends – towards becoming the person and professional we want to be. This is an important building block in creating the right sort of learning climate in the company and for providing self-development opportunities for individuals.

Here is an outline of a PDP – just one of many variations. If you like the idea, you need to develop a form that suits your company.

Learning contract
This learning contract represents an agreed commitment to development
between _____ (participant) and _____ (sponsor)
Date:

Part 1: preparation (A set of questions to help the person think through their
 needs and ambitions)

• Current job	What are your key skills and areas of strength? Which tasks do you find the most difficult? What talents are not being used in your current job? What skills/knowledge do you think you lack? . . . and so on.
• Career interests	What alternative career paths are open to you? What work areas or tasks would lead to these? How is the work/home balance for you right now? Where could you be in five years' time? . . . and so on.
• Development	What education, training or development do you need? What's happening in your out-of-work life? What talents and abilities do you want to realize more? . . . and so on.

Part 2: development plan (A list of goals with target dates, resources
needed, etc.)

Development area	Objective	Method
1. Computing, for example	1. Learn to operate, e.g., programming and keyboard skills on IBM PC's by 30 September	1. Coaching and hands-on practice
2.		
3.		
. . . and so on.		

What kind of experience, special assignments, personal improvements, educa-tion and training would be helpful in the next 12 months? (It helps here if all the resources available in the company are listed, e.g. projects, attachments, libraries, open learning materials, people willing to coach on certain skills, sources of information, seminars and courses – internal and external, career counselling and so on.)

1. Computing: attachment to Brendan Dean's office (needs negotiating; can Celeste help?)

2.
. . . and so on.

Part 3: action plan (What can I do? Who can help? Would it be helpful to contact others? Who and when?)

Actions at work	Actions outside work
1. Computing: talk to Celeste, then to Brendan and fix, say, a regular half-day per week. 2. . . . and so on.	1. 2.
Review dates	Others involved

Many companies are now using variations on the idea of PDPs and you could perhaps get examples by asking around among your contacts. Some case examples can be found in *Applying self-development in organizations* M. J. Pedler, J. G. Burgoyne and T. H. Boydell (eds) Prentice-Hall (1988).

Glimpse 37
Striving to please our members

In Chapter 2 we stressed that the company will only be successful in the long term by striving to 'delight' customers and meeting the requirements of other stakeholders. These others include suppliers, neighbours, owners, even competitors as well as employees and customers. These are the 'members' of your company in the widest sense of the word. Glimpse 25 is concerned with customers and employees, here we look at the wider world.

Brainstorm a list of the members of your company, as we have done below for Totley Kitchen Designs. Your list may include specific names and also more general clusters of people.

- Suppliers
  - Woods Timber
  - Premier Transport
  - Hardcliff Catering
  - Hallamshire Bus Company
  - Yorkshire Electricity Board
- Owners
  - All shareholders
  - Josephine Taylor ⎫
  - Jean Mann ⎭ Partners
- Neighbours
  - Duplex Manufacturing (specific company)
  - Local People (group of residents)
  - River Don; Totley Woods (environment)
  - Statutory Bodies representing neighbours
- Competitors
  - Beta Kitchens
  - Lancaster Paint Company

As your full list may be quite long, the next step is to choose some priorities. You can use various techniques to pick out the most important from each group in terms of the urgency of improving the relationship, but choose at least three from each group.

For each of your chosen members, discuss what you think would

- delight them
- please them
- satisfy them.

Rather than just talking about these points, some of you could play the roles of the various members and put *their* view.

You could give yourself a score out of ten as to how well you're doing at the moment on each of these points for each member. Then, give a qualitative description of why you gave this score. What data did you use? Again, a role play or 'interview' might give you some good ideas here.

Although it is you who needs to please your company's members, they in turn may be in a position to empower you to do so. Now identify some ways in which they could help you delight, please and satisfy them using this threefold classification:

- things you do that help me to please you – please continue or do even more of these
- things you do that make it difficult for me to please you – please do less of these or stop altogether
- things you don't do now that would help me to please you – please start to do these.

You now need to grasp the nettle of going out and talking with various members. Obviously this will need careful arranging and briefing, explaining the purpose of your visit, fixing a suitable time and place and so on.

The overall purpose of all this, of course, is to take charge of the process of continuously improving your relationships with your members. This will involve describing the whole philosophy of this approach; sharing your perception of what will delight, please or satisfy them; and, equally, sharing your picture of how well you think you are doing and what their view is of this. Once again the three headings – continue, stop, start – may be useful. Finally, you can tell them what you would find helpful from them.

Going through this process might take several meetings, especially with tricky relationships such as competitors or those with a poor history. However, watchers of the modern management scene are putting great emphasis on a company's ability to make alliances and operate in networks as a key for success, survival and learning. The structure offered here is one that you could use to design your own process and plan for making a start on developing your relationships with your members.

FOLLOW-UP READING

Harrison, R., 'When Power Conflicts Trigger Team Spirit', *European Business*, Spring (1982).

Although best known for his theory and practice of action learning (see Glimpse 45), Reg Revans has always worked with a vision of the Learning Company. His concern has always been to empower the manager struggling with intractable problems, and he sees the highest expression of action learning in the concept of the learning community or learning system.

In the little-known paper 'The Enterprise as a Learning System' Revans articulates his well-known scorn for experts and expert systems but also lays out a very modern conception on the symbiosis of work and learning:

> We observe that all expert systems here referred to must now be imposed upon the enterprise from above or from outside. But action learning must seek the means of improvement from within, indeed from the common task . . . the daily round offers constant learning opportunities . . . the quality of such learning is largely determined by the morale of the organization . . .
>
> (i) . . . that its chief executive places high among his own responsibilities that of developing the enterprise as a learning system: this he will achieve through his personal relations with his immediate subordinates . . .
> (ii) . . . maximum authority for subordinates to act within the field of its own known policies that become known by interrogation from below . . .
> (iii) . . . codes of practice . . . and other such regulations are to be seen as norms around which variations are deliberately encouraged as learning opportunities . . .
> (iv) . . . any reference to what appears an intractable problem to a superior level should be accompanied both by an explanation of why it cannot be treated where it seems to have arisen and a proposal to change the system so that similar problems arising in future could be suitably contained and treated . . .
> (v) . . . persons at all levels should be encouraged, with their immediate colleagues to make regular proposals for the study and reorganization of their own systems of work . . .

FOLLOW-UP READING

Revans, R. W., *The Origins and Growth of Action Learning*, Chartwell-Bratt (1982).

Glimpse 39
Strengths, Weaknesses, Opportunities and Threats analysis (SWOT)

SWOT (Strengths, Weaknesses, Opportunities and Threats) analysis is one of the best-known tools for helping people look at their strategic position. Usually applied to businesses, it can easily be adapted for use with groups or individuals and is perhaps best done by brainstorming or interviewing for lists of items under the four headings. Strengths and Weaknesses are to do with Looking In, while Opportunities and Threats are to do with Looking Out. Here are some questions under each of the headings to help you carry out a SWOT analysis.

Strengths	*Opportunities*
• What are you good at? • How are you doing competitively? • What are your assets in terms of people, systems, products, finance, sales, knowledge, reputation?	• What do you set out to be? • What changes do you expect to see in demand over the next five years? • What opportunities are there?
Weaknesses	*Threats*
• What do you do badly? • What weaknesses do you have in terms of people, systems, products, sales, finance, knowledge, reputation? • What annoys your customers most?	• What do other people have that you don't? • How easily can people enter your market in the future? • What changes are coming that will affect your business?

FOLLOW-UP READING

Young, A., *The Manager's Handbook*, Sphere (1986).

All learning proceeds from differences. When we notice what is different from what we expected, there is the learning opportunity. The rigorous process of science progresses via the hypothesis, then an experiment and then a careful observation of the results. New ideas come from the differences between what was expected – the hypothesis – and the actual findings. In everyday life we are usually less rigorous, yet we proceed on the basis of hypotheses or assumptions about what will happen if I do this or that. Often we are angry if our hypotheses are disproved – 'something went wrong!', we say. This judgement stops learning.

In companies there are other barriers to learning. For example, company policies set out to get everyone to act the same. Also, companies are political in the sense that people hold different views and seek to influence others to adopt their way of thinking. This political process inhibits open expression of differences and the proper debate of issues that might lead to learning. The Learning Company finds ways of becoming aware of differences – perhaps between women and men, old and young, white and black, northerners and southerners and so on – in order to free people to be different within the company, and to learn from these differences.

This requires courage. Surfacing and discussing differences means accepting and dealing with the underlying conflict. Significant learning, on the other hand, is rarely achieved without the energy and heat of such questioning, debate and conflict. Here's a simple activity for developing differences within a group or company.

- Becoming aware. List all the differences between people in the room in relation to, say, company business strategy. Some of these differences might be:
  - product orientation versus service/customer orientation
  - like to be told what to do versus like to be their own boss
  - women versus men
  - wants new job versus happy with existing job
  - wants more responsibility versus wants less responsibility
  - feels listened to versus doesn't feel listened to
  - thinks all should be involved in strategy forming versus best left to 'top management'

      – happy with existing skills/knowledge versus would like to learn new skills
      – expression of conflict causes more harm than good versus conflict is a rich source of learning

- Choose a suitable difference to debate, set a fixed time and elect a referee. Encourage people to take a position on this difference by, say, getting people to negotiate their positions on a line across the room or asking people to form groups on the basis of their basic position (A or B or 'It all depends').
- Debate the difference and its impact on, in this case, business strategy. What differences are not being taken into account? Whose interest does the present strategy serve? How could it be improved? What opportunities are we missing?
- After the debate, make sure all participants have an opportunity to debrief in smaller groups. Learning from differences can be a stressful process that may start things off in people which cannot be dealt with in the debating chamber. Counselling facilities should also be available to those who take part. These facilities may be especially useful where people are not used to expressing different opinions and experiencing the strong and complicated emotions that these give rise to. This is something that becomes more familiar, if not easier, with practise.

The Learning Company can't be created without conflict. Differences are essential to transformation – becoming aware, debating, learning and deciding are part of this process. These are new skills for many company members and finding the structures to open up yet contain differences is a key part of the art.

Glimpse 41
Story-telling

The emerging ideas of *organizational transformation* (OT) stress the importance of paying attention to the non-rational, intuitive, mythical side of life in companies. This is because the planned, reasoned approaches to organizational development are somehow not sufficient. It seems you cannot transform yourself on the basis of logic alone – some intuitive leap, a wild card, some random element is required to introduce new and unexpected variety.

For this reason, OT ideas emphasize the tales, rumours, legends, myths and dreams that people in companies use to describe their experience. Stories can produce the unexpected, illogical jumps and transformations that are the very antithesis of reason – princesses turn into pumpkins at the stroke of midnight; wardrobe doors lead to other worlds. Thinking through the metaphors, myths or stories used by people in particular companies can bring out imaginative possibilities and ways forward for that company.

The authors of an article called 'A Rumpelstiltskin Organization' use the dream of a staff member to draw out what is happening in a company. In this case, the former hero and charismatic leader is blamed for inner tensions and eventually sacked – just as in the fairy-tale the discovery of Rumpelstiltskin's name robs him of his power.

Such stories or legends only have meanings within the particular setting in which they are used. Put against the conscious, rational life of that setting they can bring out truths not previously revealed. Other examples of working with organizational stories, myths and metaphors can be found in the books of Harrison Owen.

REFERENCE AND FOLLOW-UP READING

Smith, K., and V. Simmons, 'A Rumpelstiltskin Organization: Metaphors on Metaphors in Field Research', *Administrative Science Quarterly*, 28, pages 377–392 (1983).

Owen, H., *Spirit: Transformation and Development in Organizations* and *Leadership Is*, Abbot Publishing (1987 and 1990).

Glimpse 42
Visualize your company

'Only connect', E. M. Forster's famous epigram, is perhaps the most succinct way of describing the path to the Learning Company. Because we tend to think of organizations as man-made constructions, it is hard to think of them as whole, developing organisms, yet, we are beginning to be able to see companies as groupings of interdependent people trading in an environment and these can be said to learn through trial and error, questioning and re-formulating goals, purposes and values. So, to the extent that we connect – form a whole, are mutually dependent, share a common life – we can be together, organize together and, indeed, learn together.

Even so, it's still hard to see the company as a whole being. Here's an activity that you can try by yourself, with a small group or even at a large conference, but with a large group you may need some help to organize it appropriately.

Imagine your company as a person and ask the questions
- What sort of a person is it?
- Is it female or male?
- How old is it?
- Is it thin or fat?
- What temperament is it – lively, fiery and explosive or earthy, strong and slow-moving or light, full of ideas and quick or flowing, endlessly weaving and flexible?
- What is its name?
- What is your company good at? What are its strengths? What are the weaknesses?

Glimpse 43
Breaking patterns: change your management meetings

One of the keys to the Learning Company is finding simple ways to change. Small steps are often better than large ones because they don't frighten us so much. In any case, your 'small' step – especially when you're the initiator of change – is going to be someone else's big one and perhaps even the last straw.

A friend in the police was promoted to chief superintendent in charge of a large patch containing several small towns. One of the first things he did was to introduce 'team briefing' – a 30-minute session on Monday mornings over coffee in his office for all his managers. He reflected, 'What was most surprising – and touching in a way – was how I had to teach them to talk to each other in the work setting. They were fine talking ten to the dozen in the pub after work, but they didn't know how to talk to each other informally at work'.

Because they are such a common and increasing feature of the workplace, meetings are a good place to start breaking patterns and introducing small changes. What small changes could *you* introduce to *your* meetings? Here are a few ideas you might try:

- if you usually have an agenda, try doing without one (people may start talking about what's important to them)
- change the physical setting – change the room, the seating, remove the tables
- hold your meeting off-site, but not necessarily in a hotel – why not try your home?
- end the meeting on the stroke of the agreed finishing time
- start with a poem, a story, a small meditation
- if you always have the same person in the chair, take it away from them (especially if the chair is also the boss)
- invite someone to the meeting who 'shouldn't' be there
- devise a penance for latecomers – one person we know keeps a plant spray in the office with which offenders are doused (especially senior ones), but a less boisterous idea is to have the last person make or buy the tea
- write the minutes *before* the meeting (and have people argue with them if they wish)

And so on. With a couple of confederates you could think up a dozen or more ways to make a change in your meetings. Creating the Learning Company is not just about changing meetings, of course, but you have to start somewhere. Whatever you do, the most important thing is to make some time towards the end to ask people what difference the change has made. Reviewing is as important as doing. Reflecting on differences brings us to awareness and perhaps to learning.

Glimpse 44
How to be a leader in the Learning Company

Mr Thorncliffe, the Head of Woodmill School, died at his post after 32 years in the job. Woodmill was a very private school – the teachers respected each other's space and didn't talk about work in the staffroom, sticking to subjects like homes and holidays. Probationers found it a tough school to learn in. If they asked for help, they were likely to be told 'We had to learn how to teach for ourselves!', or, 'Work it out for yourself' and they rarely stayed longer than their probationary year if they could help it.

The new Head, Mrs Ashton, brought in one or two new teachers, but she also brought some new ways of behaving. She was taking an Open University course in the teaching of reading to young children and one day she burst excitedly into the staffroom saying, 'Look at this! I've just discovered this research which shows that children look at the whole page of a book as a whole picture and not as lines of print. *We* have to teach them to follow each line along from left to right – isn't that amazing! It's so obvious! How could I have been teaching all these years without realizing that?'

While ashamed of herself for not knowing such an 'obvious' thing, Mrs Ashton was not embarrassed, she did not hide it or to let it dampen her enthusiasm for learning. This was typical of her and gradually she introduced a new atmosphere into the school.

From this little story seem to emerge three conditions for being a leader in a learning company:

- *Do it yourself* you are always engaged in learning something – what's your current learning project?
- *Share and demonstrate your new learning* when did you last make it obvious to your colleagues that you've just learned something?
- *Make learning normal, legitimize it and encourage others to do it* learning is part of life and work in the Learning Company – look around you, is it obvious that those around you are learning from what they are doing?

You can overdo it, of course. As a leader you can't *always* be asking for help, you can't behave as if you don't know anything. Openness to learning doesn't mean that you are feeble or incompetent all the time. However, many people in leadership roles in companies *do* feel a great deal of pressure to be competent all the time – and that means that they never learn anything. Worse still, because they never admit to learning or needing to, no one around them dares to teach them. Eventually you get a non-learning company – and there are too many of those already.

To be a leader in a Learning Company you have to be able to be both competent *and* incompetent.

Glimpse 45
Action learning sets

Action learning is the brainchild of Professor Reg Revans who has been one of the architects of the idea of the Learning Company for many years. Action learning is his method for personal and organizational development and involves small groups (sets), each member of which takes a difficult task or problem in the company and acts to change it, bringing the results back to the set for review and learning. As Revans has said, 'There is no learning without action and no (sober and deliberate) action without learning'.

To start an action learning set:

- recruit six people who wish to develop themselves through tackling a live, company problem, for example, increasing quality, cutting waste, improving a service
- ask each person to write a brief description of the problem to be tackled and a picture of how things will be when it is resolved – what benefits will result?
- find a sponsor or mentor for each person who can act as a company aunt or uncle, smoothing the path, giving advice and so on
- agree a programme of meetings, say half a day every two weeks or a day every month, for the group to meet, perhaps with a set adviser to manage the process and encourage members to give and take with and from each other
- at each meeting members share the time and report in turn on their efforts since the last meeting; other members help each person learn from their actions by questions and feedback, support and challenge and finally each person ends by setting goals for action by the next meeting.

This is a simple yet profound process. Only individuals prepared to give it a go and to take a risk will be able to act and learn in this way. Only companies open to learning will allow members this sort of freedom. Action learning is one of the most powerful methods of development to emerge from the 1970s and 1980s. You can make it part of a longer course, or you can have free-standing sets. These days it is getting hard to find a well-designed development programme without at least an action learning component.

FOLLOW-UP READING

If you want to follow the action learning path there are a number of sources of further information. Two of these are:

Revans, R. W., *The ABC of Action Learning*, Charwell-Bratt (1983).
Pedler, M. J., *Action Learning in Practice* (second edition), Gower Press (1991).

Glimpse 46
Self-development groups

Self-development groups differ from action learning sets (see Glimpse 45) and task forces (see Glimpse 47) in that they are not restricted to work issues – they can be helpful with anything important to members – and they are more likely to be managed and facilitated by the members themselves.

Eda set up a self-development group for herself and seven other women that she knew. Like her, three of them worked for Loxley Travel, two were friends of some standing and the other two were neighbours. Eda wanted help to sort out her life. She was interested in her career and committed to the company, but her husband Duncan and their three growing children complained that she neglected them. It was hard for Duncan to accept that she earned more than he did and had better career prospects.

Eda approached nine people in all to join her, only choosing women and asking each if she had an important question or concern that she wanted to consider in such a group. She had suggested two-weekly meetings of three hours or so, meeting in the evenings or at the weekends. One of those she approached felt she did not have the time, while another said that 'it didn't feel right for her'. Those who joined had very different concerns. Jean's husband was out of work and she had a struggle to make ends meet; Val was considering becoming a Quaker; Sylvie was trying to make up her mind whether she should leave her secure job to go freelance.

After two meetings, Eda could not imagine being without the group. She had found using her 30 minutes of 'air time' difficult at first, but afterwards found that she had moved in her thinking quite considerably. The response of the others, their own stories and even jokes at her expense, had been very revealing to her.

The group continued to meet for almost two years and, after two members left, the others held a party and celebrated the end. Although one member felt 'it hadn't done much for her, although she had enjoyed the company', everyone else felt that the group had been very significant in helping them make decisions and, more importantly, in giving them a sense that they could, to some extent, take responsibility for themselves and their lives.

FOLLOW-UP READING

Kemp, N., 'Self-development: Practical Issues for Facilitators', *Journal of European Industrial Training*, 13(5) (1989).

Pedler, M. J., 'Developing Within the Organization: Experiences with Management Self-development Groups', *Management Education & Development*, 17(1) pages 5–21 (1986).

Keatings of Mold, North Wales, is a small but rapidly expanding company that engraves cylinders for the printing of packagings of household name clients like Cadbury's and Marks and Spencer. Keatings is a breakaway from a larger company and Mike Keating, its managing director, is determined not to make some of the mistakes he experienced in the past. One view of his – echoed by many of the staff, who are all paid the same high, flat rate of pay – is that everybody should be doing the managing and that there should be no designated managers, apart from Mike and his fellow director, Phil.

Consultants carried out a survey that identified a list of ways in which the running of the company could be improved. These ranged from improving the labelling of cylinders to computerizing the ever-shifting operating schedule; from more people needing to deal with customers to designing the layout of the new building. Most of these 'needs' came from the staff and not from the directors.

As part of developing managing skills among the staff, the consultants suggested that everyone become a member of a task force with others from different parts of the factory. Although there were only 30 or so staff at this stage, there were significant differences in terms of jobs, knowledge about the whole factory and so on. Each person in each of the seven four-person task forces chose a task for themselves and sometimes the whole team took on a given task, such as designing a new building. The consultants set each group off with a two-hour session on how to work in a team and helped each task force to choose a coordinator, agree meeting times, target dates for completing tasks and so on. The task forces then met as and when they wished.

After three months, most of the tasks had been completed. A party was held to hear summary reports and to celebrate. The results were impressive – not only in terms of improved supplier quality, better customer contact, computerized planning and the other tasks, but also in terms of people's abilities and willingness to take responsibility for managing. Most people now felt that they could take on jobs and responsibilities which were outside their job definitions and make a valuable contribution.

Glimpse 48
Eco-auditing

Esprit de Corp, an American casual clothing company, recently commissioned Fritjof Capra's Elmwood Institute in Berkeley, California, to carry out an 'eco-audit' of the business. The eco-audit combines looking at the impact of the business on the outer environment, and vice versa, together with the internal relationships among the members and explores the links between inner and outer relationships.

The eco-audit is a response to the new thinking about organizational ecology that focuses research on the collaborative as well as the competitive aspects of relationships between organizations. Just as ecologists who look at nature are concerned about the disastrous effects of industrial pollution, an ecological perspective on organizations shows the potentially destructive effects of individualistic and hyper-competitive lines of action by powerful companies that threaten to make the social world unmanageable.

Organizational ecologists stress 'the survival of the fitting' as the ethics of collaboration and partnership become more dominant:

> Seen from a global viewpoint, the organization exists only as part of a larger reality, supported and nurtured by the larger system on which it depends . . . From such a viewpoint, organizational purpose is not simply decided by its members, but is, in large part, 'given' by its membership of the larger system . . . Adopting such a view requires a fundamental change in one's orientation to goals and the success or failure of one's plans . . . [We can profitably] take the view that our organization has an appropriate place in the larger system, and that our task as managers and leaders is to attune our organization to its environment in order to discover what our part is and play it. The difficulties we experience are interpreted as signs and signals from the environment that we are somehow out of resonance with our true role . . . According to this point of view it should not be difficult for an organization to survive and thrive, any more than an organ in a healthy body has to work especially hard to survive. When it plays its part it receives the nourishment it needs. From a system point of view, then, strategic thinking is a search for meaning, rather than a search for advantage. (Harrison 1983)

REFERENCE

Harrison R., 'Strategies for a New Age', *Human Resource Management*, 22(3), pages 209–235 (1983).

Glimpse 49
What is an organization?

The word 'organization' has at least two everyday meanings – first, a collection of people or a bounded entity; second, a process of ordering work.

In Glimpse 50, we see that the milkman is linked to his supplier and that if they don't deliver to him, he can't deliver to the customer. The organizing process reaches back from the customer, through the delivery system to the dairy and, ultimately, to the farmer and the cow. You could go even further in tracing the links, to the people who supply cattle feed, for example. This is to think of organization as process.

In the other sense – as bounded entities – the milk round is a small business, the dairy is another business and the farmer yet another. All these are organizations with members, boundaries, plant, property, legal liabilities and so on. You could draw a map of the organized process flows with circles showing the different individual organizations that specialize in various parts of the process.

What does this distinction mean for organizational learning?

The story of the milk round is of one bounded organization trying to learn and adapt and being blocked by another, the dairy. Both are part of the same organization as process, so this raises the question of whether you can have learning in one organization, as a bounded entity, without learning in the organization *process*? To have learning in this particular process, the dairy would have to reconsider its identity as being in the dairy as opposed to the milk business. If you're in the dairy business, soya milk is outside your scope, but if you're in the milk business, it *is* your territory.

From an organization as process point of view, organizational learning means change and development in the 'process lines'. In our example, it is conceivable that ecological, public health and animal welfare concerns might combine in questioning the validity of the food chain from the production of vegetable proteins to the consumption of cow's milk. From here you might reach the conclusion that using the cow in the food chain is more extravagant than bypassing it! This sort of questioning, related to emerging trends, gives some idea of what is involved in learning in an organization as process way.

To take the example a stage further, organizations as entities often block learning in the organization as process way. This is because of vested interest and concern for individual organizational survival. Food companies are often accused of perpetuating unhealthy practices or of holding back advances in public health and nutrition. Learning in the organization as process way can, however, create all sorts of new opportunities for business. In our example, this would be for a soya milk wholesaler and distributor to do milk rounds. When we talk of collaborative learning between organizations it is precisely this process we have in mind – of people in the organization as process getting together to learn and look for new opportunities.

This analysis helps to explain why we chose the term Learning *Company* rather than Learning *Organization* for this book. We prefer 'company' because it means people working together in each other's company, not because we have a primary concern for the private, 'for profit' sector. If we see ourselves as working and learning 'in company' with others, both in the bounded entity sense and in the organization as process sense, then we can learn from organizing in *both* senses and not be blocked by the limits of the particular boundaries of our present company.

Who we see ourselves working in company with creates and limits our opportunities. What or who is your company? Thinking of company in the organization as process sense can extend our boundaries and help us think outside our habitual frames of reference. We can see ourselves working in company with all sorts of people – it's a question of how we conceptualize it or place it. The way we see or conceptualize things leads us to do what we do or influences how we enact our notion of 'company' or 'organization'. Current themes in managerial culture stress excellence, competition and market forces rather than contemporary cultural concerns with ecology, health and animal welfare.

Although organization as process may seem at first sight the weaker idea, it can become strong if it helps us visualize the world differently. In *thinking* differently we will *act* differently and actually change things.

Border Dairies encourages its franchised milk deliverers to ask their customers from time to time what new products and services they would like from the dairy. In this way, over the years, Christmas and birthday cakes and Easter eggs have joined the long list of dairy and vegetable products that can now be bought from the milkman.

One day, Ernest Jones knocked at a door to enquire as to why there had been a drop in the milk order. He found out that two members of the household had become vegans and therefore drank only soya milk. Ernest said he would ask his sole supplier, Border, if they could get him the soya milk. In this case, Border decided that there was not enough demand to justify setting up supplies, so Ernest had to disappoint his customer.

Perhaps the dairy should have been a little more imaginative and tried to actively sell the new milk; perhaps they should have loosened their franchise agreement and let Ernest get his own supplies from elsewhere? What this little story shows is how invaluable the customer contacts of the staff can be in detecting new markets and opportunities. Those in contact with suppliers and competitors could do the same. We hear that representatives of Japanese firms are always on the lookout for ideas and practices that they can take back. It is a matter of attitude, of frame of mind, of the cultural acceptance of the possibility of learning from others.

Glimpse 51
Is this a Learning Company?

Building Designs Systems (BDS) is a company employing some 60 people, making and installing windows, doors, double glazing and conservatories in a large East Midlands town. Trade fluctuates with the demand for home improvements, which varies considerably with the level of interest rates. In the last few years, rates have risen and fallen and currently stand at a very high level.

Last Wednesday, John Porter, the caretaker/handyman was asked to come in at the very early hour of 5.00 a.m. to open the offices and workshops. Outside were three furniture vans and all the staff were on hand to help with the removal of 90 per cent of the stock and work in progress, together with most of the office equipment and furniture. At 6.45 a.m. the vans drove away and the staff dispersed to have breakfast. At 8.00 a.m. the liquidator arrived to value the inventory and the company. At 10.30 a.m. the liquidator left and at 12.00 noon the vans returned and were unloaded by the staff. By 1.00 p.m. BDS was trading as Cosmopolitan Homes Ltd, a new company with new directors. All the staff were working as normal on their customary low wages and with the usual warnings of dismissal if they contemplated joining trades unions – nothing had changed.

During the afternoon, John discovered from one of the older hands that this was not the first time this had happened. A very similar exercise had taken place some 5 years previously, although then some 20 staff had lost their jobs that time. Then the company had been called Grosvenor Windows Ltd, but the management had stayed the same throughout. This explained why it was often difficult to get supplies and why different workers were sent considerable distances to open new accounts.

Is this a Learning Company? It is flexible and adaptable and certainly has learned one way of dealing with market fluctuations, but is it a Learning Company?

Glimpse 52
Sock on the wrong foot?

Thanks to information technology, the Sock Shop is reputedly able to inspect the day's trading figures from all its branches two hours after the close of business. Visions of lorry loads of socks being despatched to snow-bound areas? But Sock Shop, along with other niche marketers, got into financial troubles through a combination of rapid growth, high rental outlets and a fall in impulse purchasing with the downturn in disposable income.

With the 20:20 vision of hindsight, what kind of management information system might help to anticipate these sorts of trends and identify appropriate courses of action to avert disaster?

Glimpse 53
Saved by a form

Everyone works hard at Richardson's and gives every appearance of enjoying life, including the two owners, who are always around, always accessible. Yet, although this small office supplies firm was expanding, they never seemed to be able to hang on to enough revenue to get the new warehouse they sorely needed.

Discussions showed that they didn't really know which orders they made money on: they couldn't tell the high value-added orders from the ones that made little or no contribution. If the accountant didn't know, then how could anyone else?

After some thought, a new order form was produced for the reps. Based on the known fixed cost of any delivery and the cost of assembling the order (roughly proportional to the variety of items in it), three lines were added to the order form. The new form enabled the rep to work out the business value of any order they took. There was no rule about not accepting orders below a certain value, because the firm was committed to a long-term view of the customer relationship and would deliver what was asked for, it was simply that the new form made the reps and everyone else aware of their most valuable customers, actually and potentially.

It was very simple. It was very 'low-tech'. It worked.

Glimpse 54
Fighting about what's important

It's quite clear that being in a Learning Company does not make for a quiet life. In adults and in mature organizations learning is always associated with a certain amount of upset, of giving up old ways to take on new ones. The Learning Company is one that, every now and again, is able to challenge its own operating assumptions, its very taken for granted ways of doing things. It's obvious that this cannot be done without conflict and argument.

Conflict can be creative, starting from differences among us and leading to all of us seeing things differently – when we manage to find the 'third position', or, the synthesis of the argument and counter-argument. Yet it can also be destructive, leading to unresolved difficulties, running battles, stand-offs or insidious undercurrents that haunt us in the future. The Learning Company has to find ways of encouraging more of the former and less of the latter. Perhaps it's not so much a question of having 'constructive conflicts' as having the attitude that causes us to ask the questions, 'Why are we in conflict?' and 'What can we learn from it?' (see Figure G54.1). This takes maturity and learning in itself.

The level of conflict is high in 'adolescence', when shared understanding is low, and decreases with age. However, as the Learning Company reaches a certain stage of maturity it can tolerate and cope with *more* conflict where differences are appropriately surfaced and worked on to produce double loop learning or organizational transformation.

In this model, education plays a crucial part in converting conflict into learning. In adolescence, education focuses upon helping everyone learn the 'language' and skills of managing with others. This learning forms an essential infrastructure that enables learning and transformation from differences and conflict.

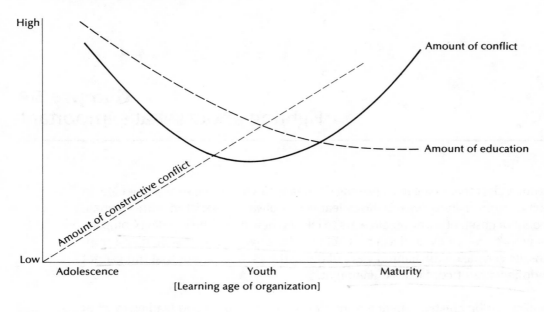

Figure G54.1 Learning from conflict

REFERENCE

This idea came to us from Nick Georgiades in Pedler, M. J., T. H. Boydell and J. G. Burgoyne, *Learning Company Project Report*, Training Agency, Sheffield, p. 23 (May 1988).

Marks and Spencer's suppliers

M & S are reputed to have a strong and demanding influence on their suppliers. Rigorous quality control standards are applied and monitoring procedures reach deep into suppliers' operations.

Suppliers are said to have mixed reactions to this, though not too mixed or too public if they wish to stay suppliers. The exacting standards do improve their quality, but sometimes too much so for their other markets. There are feelings of loss of control and of being trapped into dependency, yet they have achieved the status of No. 1 supplier on the high street. Suppliers certainly learn things from M & S, but is there a flow of learning in the other direction?

These are some of the dynamics of interorganizational relationships and learning.

Glimpse 56
Integrated operations

The windscreen manufacturing plant is on the car assembly site, but it belongs to a glass firm and not to the motor manufacturer. Just in time delivery systems and a TQM regime stitch the two together pretty completely. Staff in the glass plant are employees of the glass firm but culturally and day-to-day are part of the car assembly plant. Career planning and other aspects of managing are dealt with jointly and both the glass firm and the car manufacturer learn from practices that they would not normally experience.

Some of this learning is 'exported' to other parts of their businesses. It's a bonus that was not anticipated when the integrated plant was set up. The Learning Company sets out deliberately to learn from such collaborative relationships.

There is a debate in the corporate strategy literature as to whether strategy forma-tion is a regular, systematic process of taking stock, reviewing and setting new directions or whether it is a process that happens only when 'big decisions' have to be made.

Pilkington's recently made a 'big decision' about where to locate a new float glass plant. The options were St Helens, Pilkington's traditional home base, or Kent, to take advantage of the Channel tunnel and the continental European market. There were plenty of arguments on both sides. The business logic was for Kent, but land and labour are cheaper in Lancashire. If the company did *not* site in Kent, perhaps a continental manufacturer would operate from the other end of the tunnel and get a competitive advantage in the lucrative southern UK market. On the other hand, Pilkington's have a long tradition, with some ups and downs, of being a big and good local employer, taking their social responsibility seriously.

The issue was widely debated internally to get the widest possible view and gain commitment, especially during internal management programmes and other gatherings. On the whole, the Kent option gained ground – it made more business sense, even if it did create local difficulties – and then a funny thing happened.

The Board announced that the plant would be built in St Helens and, indeed, that implementation plans were well advanced and would go forward quickly. It was an odd experience for those who had endlessly discussed the pros and cons and who had come to accept that it might have to be Kent. Had it been the tradition or cheapness of St Helens that had tipped the balance?

As with many such tales, we are never likely to arrive at a single truth or even a balanced account of the experiences and perceptions of making a big decision. In a sense that doesn't matter because what we have here is an illustration of the complexities of strategic decision making and the dilemmas that can follow the Learning Company approach of consulting and involving as many people as possi-ble. Three points emerge, however, from this story that are of particular importance for those who are concerned in realizing the Learning Company:

- there is a very real dilemma in balancing the wish to be a 'good company', as an employer and a contributor to the local economy, with the need to be a successful and competitive company
- there is a conflict between the demands for openness and for broad participation in decision making with the inevitable need for some confidentiality and secrecy about strategic plans in a competitive situation
- participation takes time and people must be given time to work out what they think in consultation with others; equally there are times when there is a need to be decisive and to act quickly in order to 'hit the ground running'.

The challenge for the Learning Company is to find ways of combining a commitment to broad participation and consultation with both the necessary confidentiality and the need for speed.

Getting the POWer into the Learning Company

Here are three simple pictures of

* the non-Learning Company (Figure G58.1) where the owners/managers decide on the outputs or goals and these remain unchanged by the organizing process

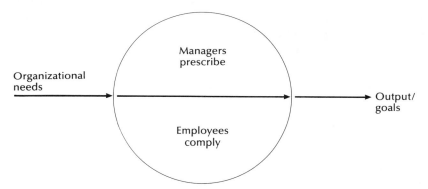

Figure G58.1 The non-Learning Company

* the single loop Learning Company (Figure G58.2) where the original needs are modified and changed in the process of organizing to produce outputs and sometimes new outputs and new ways of achieving them are the result of this learning

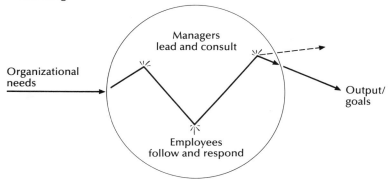

Figure G58.2 The single loop Learning Company

149

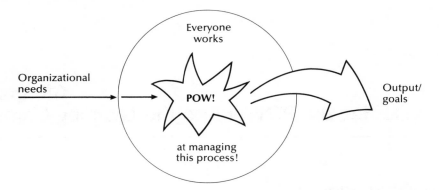

Figure G58.3 The double loop Learning Company

- the double loop Learning Company (Figure G58.3) where the 'era of stable performance' that characterize non-Learning Companies and single loop Learning
Companies is replaced with chaos and breakdown in the existing order and an
enormous surge of energy and power!

Peters and Waterman on the Learning Company

Perhaps the most influential management text of the last decade was *In Search of Excellence* by T. J. Peters and R. H. Waterman. The Learning Company goes beyond the idea of excellence to make *learning* the central process. Continuous improvement and never finally arriving are now the order of the day. However, Peters and Waterman were very concerned with adaptability, responsiveness and learning:

> The excellent companies are learning organizations.

What do they mean by this?

> They experiment more, encourage more tries and permit small failures; they keep things small; they interact with customers – especially sophisticated customers – more . . . they encourage internal competition and allow resultant duplication and overlap; and they maintain a rich informal environment, heavily laden with information, which spurs diffusion of ideas that work. Interestingly very few are articulate about what they're up to . . . They know it when they see it . . . but they . . . have no sound language with which to describe the phenomenon.

Though they couldn't then articulate it, experimenting and making mistakes (but only right ones!) are the heart of Peters' and Waterman's vision of the Learning Company:

> . . . we believe that the truly adaptive organization evolves in a very Darwinian way. The company is trying lots of things, experimenting, making the right sorts of mistakes; that is to say, it is fostering its own mutations. The adaptive corporation has learned quickly to kill off the dumb mutations and invest heavily in the ones that work.

You can't go it alone; you do it with customers:

> . . . the process of mutant generation (experiments, tries, mistakes) . . . occurs via a remarkably rich set of interactions with the environment – namely customers.

REFERENCE

Peters, T. J. and R. H. Waterman, *In Search of Excellence: Lessons from America's Best-Run Companies*, Harper & Row (1982), page 110 *et seq.*

Glimpse 60
Deming on the Learning Company

W. Edwards Deming is the most radical of the TQM gurus, recognizing not only the basic principles, such as negotiating customer–supplier needs, measurement, continuous improvement and so on, but also emphasizing that total quality requires fundamental shifts in the way we manage and organize.

This is clear from his famous 14 points:

- create constancy of purpose for improvement of product and service, with the aim of becoming competitive, staying in business and providing jobs
- adopt the new philosophy: we are in a new economic age, created by Japan; western management must awaken to the challenge, must learn their responsibilities, and take on leadership for a change
- cease dependence on inspection to achieve quality, eliminate the need for inspection on a mass basis by building quality into the products in the first place
- improve constantly and forever every activity in the company to build quality and productivity and to drive down costs
- remove barriers
  - that rob hourly workers of their right to pride of workmanship – the responsibility of supervisors must be changed from sheer numbers to quality
  - that rob people in engineering and in management of their right to pride of workmanship, which means, *inter alia*, abolition of the annual merit rating and of management by objectives
- drive out fear, so that everyone may work effectively for the company
- break down barriers between departments – people in research, design, sales and production must work as a team to foresee problems that may be encountered with the product or service
- eliminate slogans, exhortations and targets for the workforce asking for zero defects and new levels of productivity – such exhortations only create adversarial relationships; the bulk of the causes of low quality and productivity belong in the system and thus lie beyond the power of the workforce to rectify
- eliminate work standards (in the sense of numerical quotas), management by objectives, any management by numbers – substitute leadership

- institute leadership – the aim of leadership being to help people, machines and gadgets to do a better job
- institute training on the job, including (but not exclusively for) management
- institute a vigorous programme of training and self-improvement
- end the practice of awarding business on the basis of the price tag: purchasing must be combined with the design of the product; manufacturing and sales must work with chosen suppliers – the aim is to minimize total cost, not merely initial cost – move towards a single supplier for any one item on a long-term relationship of loyalty and trust
- put everyone in the company to work to accomplish the transformation; the transformation is everyone's job.

REFERENCE AND FOLLOW-UP READING

Deming, W. E., *Out of the Crisis*, Cambridge University Press (1986).
Sherkenbach, W. W., *The Deming Route to Quality and Productivity*, Ceepress Books (1986).

Glimpse 61
Deming's provocative sayings

In some ways Deming resembles Reg Revans: both are octogenarians, iconoclasts and radicals; they also both started with numbers – one as a mathematician, one as a statistician – and ended up with very different messages. This activity lists a number of Deming's one-liners and a method for using these. This activity can be used with any group of people in the company as part of a meeting or a training session to heighten awareness and share experience of Total Quality ideas.

Write each of the following of Deming's provocative sayings onto a file card:
- 'Crushed by their best efforts'
- 'All new knowledge always comes from outside'
- 'Because nothing's wrong, doesn't mean everything is right'
- 'Competition does not help the development of people'
- 'We're being ruined by people doing their best'
- 'Anyone can save money; what does it do for the company?'
- 'Exchange of ideas doesn't mean developing knowledge'
- 'Competition always leads to people being crushed'
- 'The best players don't join orchestras'
- 'Survival is not compulsory'

You can add to these if you like by using statements from Deming's 14 points given in Glimpse 60.

Each person in the group takes a card and takes it in turn to interpret its meaning in the context of their experience in the company.

FOLLOW-UP READING

Hodgson, A., 'Deming's Never-ending Road to Quality', *Personnel Management* (July 1987).
Price, F., *Right First Time and Right Every Time*, Gower (1984 and 1989).

Glimpse 62
Motorola U

Ten years ago Motorola realized that they needed people who would work for quality and output rather than the time clock. The rules of manufacturing were changing and yet the company was trying to compete globally in new technologies with people who often couldn't read adequately – only 40 per cent of the people in one plant could answer the question 'Ten is what per cent of 100?'

Motorola then launched an ambitious scheme of education and training for its employees – a scheme that they have now extended not only to all their people worldwide, but also to employees of suppliers, of principle customers and even to those of educational partners. This has built up over the ten years with many mistakes on the way, one of which was the attempt to put 400 executives through an MBA in four weeks!

Calling it a 'University' seemed ambitious, but Motorola operates with a wide range of educational partners who resource and credit the programmes and whose attitudes to collaboration with business had to change along the way. The definition of company training changed as it became not just for the company and the job but also for the person. The commitment is to:

> Creating an environment for learning, a continuous openness to new ideas . . . We not only teach people how to respond to new technologies, we try to commit them to the goal of anticipating new technologies . . . We not only teach skills, we try to breathe the very spiral of creativity and flexibility into manufacturing and management.

REFERENCE

Wiggenhorn, W., 'Motorola U: When Training becomes an Education', *Harvard Business Review*, pages 71–83 July/August (1990).

Glimpse 63
Exploring the dimensions of the Learning Company

There's a lot of exploratory work to be done in the Learning Company. Creating different options for action and debating their respective merits is an activity everyone can become skilled at given time. Many people in companies are not used to being asked for their opinions – especially when this concerns the future direction of the enterprise. However, to develop a Learning-Company approach to business strategy, it is important to get people involved if they are also to be committed to the decisions made.

Here is a simple activity that involves asking people for their opinions, and having them work in groups to come up with agreed actions.

- Ask any number of people to divide into two groups – A and B. If there are more than, say, ten in each group, then ask them to split again, giving two group As and Bs. It doesn't matter how many of each there are.
- Now brainstorm as follows:
  - *Group A*: 'What would you do, or build in, to facilitate learning in this company?' List your responses, then score each of them on a scale from 0 to 7 on how well we are doing with regard to these as a company at the moment.
  - *Group B*: What would you do, or build in, if you were trying to inhibit learning in this company? List your responses, then score each of these on a scale from 0 to 7 on how well we are doing with regard to these as a company at the moment.
- Bring groups A and B together and have each present to the other. Give each ten minutes to dispute the findings of the other (or to add to them). Now create an agreed list of recommendations for action. What would be the next steps? Do you build on positives or act to remove inhibitors?

Musical chairs is an exciting and cruel game played with equal gusto at children's parties and in the Prime Minister's Cabinet. As long as we have hierarchies in organization life, we are likely to experience our own version of musical chairs from time to time. If you get the last seat, don't you feel, oh, so pleased – and relieved, but how crushing it is to find a full company with no place for you.

The idea of the Learning Company is that *everyone* finds a seat and gets a say, but what sort of a voice you have depends a lot on how the chairs are set. Figure G64.1 gives just four ways of arranging the chairs, which affect quite strongly how most of us are likely to participate.

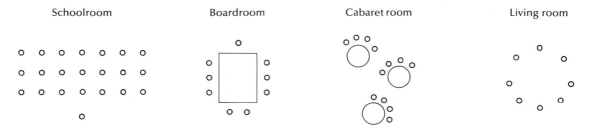

Figure G64.1 Seating plans

Jot down against each of these settings three ways in which you think your actions would be influenced by the way the furniture has been arranged.

Next time you organize a meeting with your project team or group, why not try a little organizational restructuring of your own?

- Try a new seating arrangement – there are lots of variations.
- Note the effect it has on people and how you do business together.
- Discuss why you made the change – this is how we learn!

Remember, the Learning Company starts with small steps that we can learn from together. Some of the ways you can introduce change are right under your nose.

Glimpse 65
Form follows function

One of the most common errors in making changes in organizations is when the new manager changes the structure and hopes that this will solve the problems. It rarely does. There is much to be said for changing structures, but only when the reasons for doing so have been carefully thought through, after everyone has been consulted and, preferably, after all of us have had a go at rehearsing or practising any changes in actions and behaviour that will be called for under the new structure. As in all good architectural practice – form follows function.

In their manual on making cultural changes, M. George, P. Hawkins and A. McLean offer the following model of cultural change (Figure G65.1):

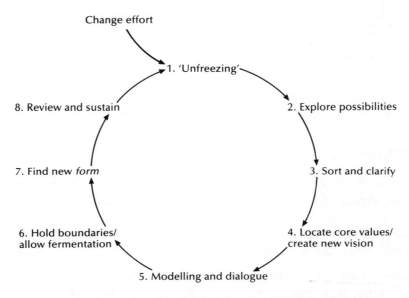

Figure G65.1 George, Hawkins and McLean's model of cultural change

Before you make any changes in your company, remember these seven steps should be gone through *before* you fix a new structure.

158

REFERENCE

George, M., P. Hawkins and A. McLean, *Organisation Culture Manual*, Bath Associates, Bath (1989).

Glimpse 66
Developing with and from the environment

Doing new things is a way of life in the Learning Company. Inventing new products, exploring new markets, experimenting with new structures or methods of working, creating new relationships, having fresh insights – all these activities provide the food for learning.

One critical element in all learning is that of *difference*. Once we notice a difference – in performance, in attitude, in outlook – it provides us with the question 'Why?', which can lead to a new idea. People outside our organization are a rich source of differences. In the Learning Company we don't just buy from suppliers, sell to our customers, compete with competitors; we set out to learn with and from them.

This requires quite a change of attitude. '*Learn* with *competitors*! . . . surely that's madness!' you might say at first, but think again – think of all those antique shops on the same street, or all those software houses in the same science park. These companies are competing in a serious way, but they also collaborate. They watch each other carefully, attempt to outdo each other certainly, but also get together from time to time to attempt projects that require the resources of two or three.

It's much the same story with customers and suppliers. If you're just seeing these people as buyers and sellers, you're missing something vital. They could be learning partners too. For example, when Austin Rover set up its 'Preferred Supplier' programme some years ago and reduced the list of over 1000 suppliers by two-thirds or so, as part of this programme they also held 'Buyer-Supplier Negotiating Training Workshops' where people formerly regarded as 'the enemy' were given free places to learn how to negotiate better with Austin Rover's buyers. Doesn't make sense does it?

It goes without saying that, for the front-line troops in many organizations, the customers, often referred to as the punters, are 'the enemy'.

Here are some questions that might help you improve your ability to learn from those outside your organization:

• What new markets have you created this year?

- What innovations, suggested by staff, have been implemented this year?
- What services and products have remained unchanged over the last five years?
- What did you learn from your last visit to a supplier?
- How many joint customer action teams do you have with existing customers?
- When was the last time you set up a joint venture with a competitor?
- With which of your suppliers do you have quality improvement projects?
- What changes have you made as a result of listening to your customers' suggestions?
- How can you involve your customers in helping you with marketing and market research?
- What changes have you made in your own life in the last year?

In the Learning Company we don't just *exist* in our environment we set out to develop it and thereby to develop ourselves.

Glimpse 67
Companies that belong to the planet

What does your company do? To whom does it belong? These look like pretty straightforward questions don't they. Perhaps most of us would say something like 'This company exists to make profit for the shareholders' or 'This company exists to provide a service to rule and belongs to the Local Authority' – what would you say?

Roger Harrison is one of the more interesting thinkers about organizations and he has recently developed a hierarchy of purposes that borrows from Maslow's famous model and takes it further (Figure G67.1):

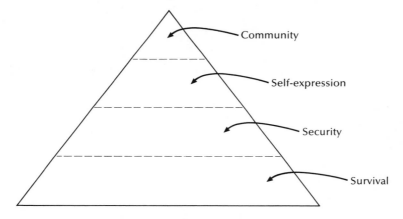

Figure G67.1 Harrison's development of Maslow's organizational model

Making a profit or delivering a service to customers is a necessary fact of existence. If this is *just* what we do then we are operating at the survival, or perhaps the security, level, but what then are the 'profit' and the 'service' for? What purpose do they serve? Now that we have refined our genius for organizing to the extent that we have, perhaps we can be a little more ambitious?

The Learning Company, like the developing person, needs to survive and have a degree of security over their lifespan, but a good quality of life demands some opportunity for self-expression. What am I here for? What can I do? What is my contribution? If as companies we are skilful and fortunate enough to survive and prosper, then what do we offer that no one else can? What contribution can we make?

Ambitious Learning Companies will want to ask further questions, such as 'Now we know what it is that we do well, that which is our special contribution, what impact does this have on the community?' and 'What value do we add to the wider world?'

Does your company just belong to the shareholders or does it also belong to the planet? What value do you really add?

FOLLOW-UP READING

Harrison, R., 'Strategies for a New Age', *Human Resource Management* 22(3) (Fall 1983). (Unfortunately, Roger Harrison hasn't written up his latest ideas in an easily accessible form, but this will give you a flavour.)

Glimpse 68
The company mobile

A family therapist we know has a mobile of a family hanging in her consulting room. There's mum and dad, the kids, grandma, aunt and dad's brother. When you pull on any one of them, the rest of them jump up and down.

Companies resemble families in that they are patterns of interaction, communication and relationship. Anything that disturbs or excites one part of the company can be felt in all the other parts. When things are going well in the company – when we find a new customer or reach a long-sought ambition – then it is a cause of celebration for all of us. When one of us dies, it is a loss to us all and we stop for a while to remember and mark the point. When things are going less well, we care less that department B is in trouble – perhaps we don't get on with them or they are making life hard for us – but, just as in the family, if we say or do something mean to them, it spreads out insidiously among the rest of us. If things get *really* bad we might call in a 'company doctor' or organization consultant to restore our well-being.

As an individual it's very hard to be conscious of the whole company when you are working by yourself or in your immediate work group. Most of the time our consciousness is limited to our own needs and those of our close colleagues. In the Learning Company we take time to try and become conscious of the whole. How are we? What's going on with everyone else? How are we organized for living and learning?

This is a hard discipline that takes time and practice to dwell on because we are so unused to thinking in terms of the whole. Yet, it's one of the keys to the Learning Company – getting the whole into every part. The ecologists' slogan 'Think global; act local' makes this same point. We have to think how can we be mindful of the whole company while getting on with the job.

Not for the first time we commend Gareth Morgan (1986) *Images of Organization* Sage (1986), especially Chapter 4 where he discusses the 'holographic' idea of organizations. Holograms are images in which every piece contains the whole – if a hologram is broken, it can be re-created from just one tiny piece.

Glimpse 69
Returning to the goddess

In the current era, many of our companies are predominantly male. This is reflected most obviously in top management – whatever the composition of the members – and also in the way we do things. Drive, single-minded commitment, toughness, competitiveness and dominance tend to be valued more than awareness, receptivity, creativity and a sense of interconnectedness and wholeness. For these reasons most companies are not able to make use of the talents of the many people who find these ideals barren and the atmosphere that results unforgiving.

Some companies are making efforts to redress this imbalance by offering Equal Opportunities programmes to increase the number of women managers or by running 'Women and Men as Working Colleagues' programmes to help men and women relate with each other effectively in the workplace. These are useful small steps but they will scarcely brush the surface unless female qualities are welcomed into the company in a more fundamental way.

The Learning Company is one that renews itself continuously. It is always learning from what it is doing. It is always giving up old ways and adopting new ones. It does not subscribe to the notion of 'never change a winning team' because it is never satisfied with any current definition of what 'winning' might mean. A Learning Company is a living company, deeply aware of the rhythms of life processes, aware of the rhythmic cycle of new life, of fecundity and death that marks all of nature.

This rhythmic cycle has been forgotten in our modern companies, striving for immortality, resisting death at all costs. In the Learning Company, death or closure or stopping doing this or that, is not an unmentionable, but an everyday occurrence. Traditionally goddesses have been concerned with the life cycle – or birth, new life; of maturity, fecundity and of wisdom; of death, which makes new life possible. To embody these essential rhythms in the Learning Company means a return to a respect for such feminine values.

FOLLOW-UP READING

Whitmont, E. C., *Return of the Goddess*, Routledge (1983).

Glimpse 70
Energy and structure

If organizing is about making the most of the available energy, what's the best structure for output and learning? This is a preoccupation in the Learning Company because energy is fluid, unpredictable, up and down, ever-changing, while structure has a tendency to ossify, to become rigid and restraining where only recently it was facilitating. Without walls and channels energy spills everywhere and is wasted, dissipated.

Plotting energy *with* structure (Figure G70.1) gives us four main possibilities, each of which has its positive and negative features.

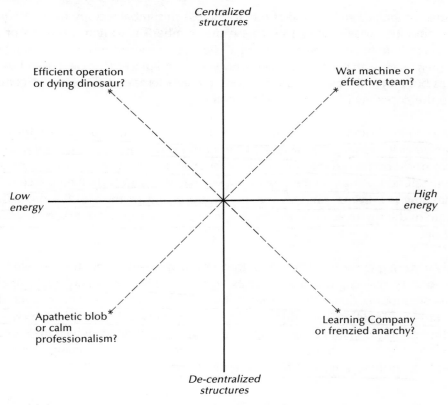

Figure G70.1 Combining energy and structure for learning

Can you place your company on the map? Where were you three years ago? Where will you be in three years' time? You can also plot departments and units separately – what happens to hot spots in dinosaurs or calm professionals in war machines?

Glimpse 71
Temporary organizations

Temporary parts in permanent wholes are one way of maintaining creativity and innovation. 'Behind the Beat' is a black music programme screened on BBC 2 and, though 'Aunty BBC' is an old, permanent company with many bureaucratic features, the production team for Behind the Beat is very temporary and fluid.

The 17 team members of 'Behind the Beat' were recruited on three-month contracts – 11 of them are new to the programme, 6 are new to TV. Terry, the creator of the programme is 26 and a good people manager and developer. To help him he has Jenny, an executive director in her 40s, to provide some wisdom and links to the parent BBC. There is ample evidence of parental feeding – people who bring telephones, photocopiers; people who provide studios and technicians; managers who provide budgets and other managers who buy the finished programmes.

The team don't have time to worry about all this. They have to learn very quickly how to do their jobs of researcher, production assistant, director or office support. They are also very aware that 'by Christmas they'll be on the streets'. They must do good work and develop their existing skills for the future. Everyone lives and works together in a big open-plan room, clustered into little groups of two and three desks. People move about frequently, try ideas out on each other, ask for contacts, call for help. On the morning after the programme goes out, Terry calls a two-hour review meeting – the only team meeting – in which the programme is picked over. Apart from initiating discussion, Terry doesn't say a lot. People who were responsible for clips ask for feedback, get praised and criticized and think about how they could do it differently.

Throughout the three months, everyone is acutely aware of time. The time of the day, the day of the week and the 'long' cycle of birth, maturity and death of the team. By Christmas the team has had its celebration and also mourned the tragic and unexpected death of one of its members.

Glimpse 72
Learning and competitive advantage

In his books, *Competitive Strategy* and *Competitive Advantage*, Michael Porter suggests that there are three basic competitive strategies:

- innovation
- quality enhancement
- cost reduction

To pursue these strategies, you need very different methods and actions on the part of the people in the company. For example, for innovation you need individual autonomy and a high level of risk taking, whereas for cost reduction you need tight control, no experiments and predictable behaviour. A Learning Company may well pursue all three strategies at different times, or all three strategies at the same time in different parts of the operation, but it is always centrally concerned with innovation.

Some companies have taken creative steps to encourage as many people as possible to take risks and innovate and get out of the habit of asking for permission and waiting for instructions. For example, 3M developed an informal norm that workers 'bootlegged' 15 per cent of their time to work on their own projects. Honda have instituted a competition for inventions among employees. Individuals or work groups submit schemes to a committee that awards time and resource budgets to projects and an annual fair is held to show off the ideas and award prizes.

We asked a group of 20 professional workers in a large service business what they saw as essential for a climate of innovation. Here are some of their comments:

- planning and review are critical activities
- no secrets, only openness
- general interest and understanding of what we're doing and what our products are
- a good methodology/capacity for self-diagnosis
- people set their own boundaries and choose their own work problems
- there is freedom *not* to learn
- a cooperative climate and equality of participation in decisions
- people take responsibility for decisions

- questions are encouraged
- people are encouraged to try things out
- people get supported for taking risks
- being excited about expanding myself – moving from spotty youth to mature human being
- no deviants!
- eliminate waste/recycle as much as possible
- lots of other people to learn with, learning partners, networks *and* teachers
- no punishments for asking questions.

These are the conditions that these people saw as enhancing their creativity and which were likely to lead to higher levels of innovation and learning. Such conditions probably wouldn't help much with cost reduction and only some of them would be useful in quality enhancement.

Here are some questions for strategists:

- What is your competitive strategy?
- Have you told other people what it is?
- Have you asked them what conditions would best support their efforts to realize this strategy?

REFERENCES

Porter, M. E., *Competitive Strategy*, The Free Press (1980)
Porter, M. E., *Competitive Advantage*, The Free Press (1985).

Glimpse 73
Multi-skilling: learning with and from workmates

Multi-skilling increases our ability to flex and adapt quickly. Combining the push towards multi-skilling with harnessing people's capacities to be both teachers or coaches and learners with each other is one hallmark of the Learning Company.

You've already met Keatings (in Glimpse 47), a rapidly expanding photo-gravure company in North Wales. As in most firms, there is a technical logic of the order in which tasks must be completed that influences the work flow. One of the critical points in this flow is the Ohio – a magical computer-controlled engraving machine that can be left to cut away all night. Only a few people know how to use it, and they went to America to learn, but others would like to learn. There it sits in its glass room, separated from the dirt and noise of the plant, always on display, central to the work process.

A list of all the jobs in the plant was drawn up, such as film making, engraving, proofing, plating as well as accounting, sales and customer relations. Each person was asked to rate themselves regarding these jobs in four categories:

- learner
- competent worker
- craftsperson
- master craftsperson/coach.

Those who were really expert at the job in question were invited to become coaches and given tuition in coaching skills. Those who want to learn a given job are encouraged to find a coach and set up agreed times for learning. These can be short full-time attachments, but are more usually small amounts of time each day or on a regular weekly basis.

At Keatings, everyone who wants to be is a learner *and* a coach.

Glimpse 74
Building the learning community

It is most infuriating when, having finally resolved some expensive problem, someone from another part of the business says, 'Oh, we could have told you how to do that!' Yet, this is a common phenomenon: much needed know-how exists just around the corner, but you didn't know that and perhaps you didn't ask. How can we get to know what is available in the way of knowledge, and skills throughout the company? How can we avail people struggling with knotty problems of the immense array of know-how and expertise in the business?

A learning community exercise may help. Here, 12 to 30 members meet on a given theme, say, pay, motivation and morale, over, say, two days, off-site. They identify and post up their needs – what they need to help them do their jobs better, to resolve the problems facing them, to overcome current blocks to progress and development. Members also work on and post up their offers – what they know, what they can do, that may be of value to others in this field and which they are prepared to put on offer.

Needs and offers are posted on a notice board and members may then make contracts to match their needs with appropriate offers. The structure is free-form and tends towards the chaotic. There is a 'free market' in needs and offers and market regulation is created only by the actions of members. Therefore, it helps to have a facilitator or two – encouraging people to be less bashful in putting forward offers, to be proactive in setting up meetings, picking up the lost and lonely and, also, once a day or so, calling a meeting to collectively review progress.

Surprising connections can be made in a learning community. Minor miracles of going to fulfil a contract on an offer you have made and mysteriously finding that one of your own needs is met in so doing. Above all people become aware of the richness of the environment surrounding them – the knowledge, the skills, the opportunities.

A word of warning, though. People have to be *ready* for a learning community. The climate has to be one where people are willing to be open and to share their ideas and experience. They also have to be able to cope with this level of messiness. Beyond and above any learning on the actual theme chosen, the learning community can help members learn to cope with 'chaos' and to be self-directing while also trying to be conscious of the whole.

FOLLOW-UP READING

Megginson, D. F. and M. J. Pedler, 'Developing Structures and Technology for the Learning Community', *Journal of European Training*, 5(5) (1976).

Glimpse 75
The strategic staircase

Strategy works backwards. Once you have a vision, a star to steer by, you can construct a strategy to get you there. The essential thing to grasp is that you work out your strategy going *backwards* from your vision and not from here forwards.

In this very simple four-step version of the strategic staircase (Figure G75.1), you start with your vision of your company as a Learning Company – what does it look like to you? Now put a time frame on it – when do you want to arrive there? Now come backwards 'down the stairs' – to get to your vision by then, what do you have to do by this date, and this date? Finally, where are you now in terms of your vision? At the moment you are on the bottom step.

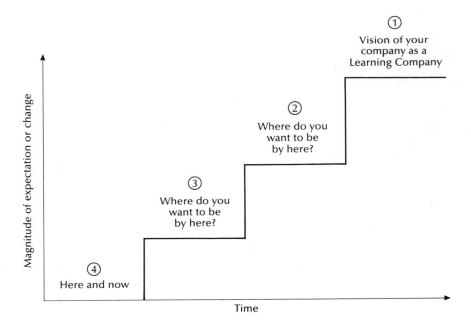

Figure G75.1 The strategic staircase

Charles Handy tells an interesting story of a cultural contrast between British and Japanese managers. It concerns the different attitudes taken to spending time on development with increasing seniority and is graphically illustrated in Figure G76.1.

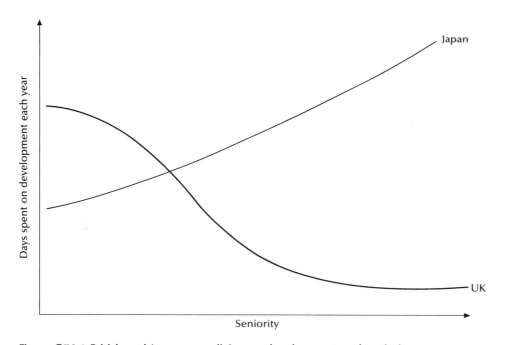

Figure G76.1 British and Japanese policies on development and seniority

If further explanation is needed, the suggestion is that as UK managers become more senior, they see themselves, and are seen to be, less in need of development. In Japan, we are told, senior managers have the contrary view: the more senior, the more need there is for development.

Glimpse 77
Personal and company learning cycles

It is interesting to note how many processes in organizations are described in cycles.

- The learning cycle (Kolb 1984) of concrete experience, reflective observation, abstract conceptualization and active experimentation.
- The task performance cycle – aim, plan, do and review.
- The training cycle of identifying needs, design, deliver and evaluate.
- The appraisal or performance review cycle – agree targets, perform, appraise and reset targets.
- Budgeting and operational planning cycles of plan/forecast, perform, monitor, review and re-plan.
- The strategic planning cycle of collect data, review situation, consider options, choose direction, direct operations, monitor and re-direct.

These cycles can be represented as concentric circles as shown in Figure G77.1.

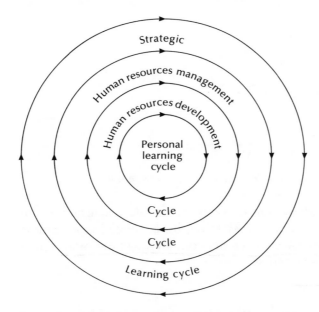

Figure G77.1 Personal and company learning cycles

One way of thinking about the Learning Company is to see it as one in which all these cycles work in harmony. In highly competitive, 'war machine'-type organizations, there is often a good deal of alignment but not much attunement. In many companies these cycles may be working independently of one another and they may even be working against each other.

REFERENCE

Kolb, D. A., *Experiential Learning*, Prentice-Hall (1984).

Glimpse 78
The company clutch plate

In Glimpse 77 we described some common cycles in corporate life and remarked on the great similarity between them. A Learning Company might be one in which these cycles are sensitively attuned with one another as well as appropriately aligned.

Here is a possible 'conductor' role for the Human Resource Development people – to orchestrate these cycles, individually and severally, to bring the company in tune, performing at its best.

Looked at this way, Human Resource Development can occupy a strategic role, mediating between personal and organizational processes, linking them and acting as 'the company clutch plate' (Figure G78.1) in bringing the energy and direction of the two kinds of processes into alignment with one another and to the point when they are properly attuned. Without the strategic clutch, the cycles of individual learning and performance are unconnected with the cycles of strategic planning and operations management with a consequent massive loss of potential and power.

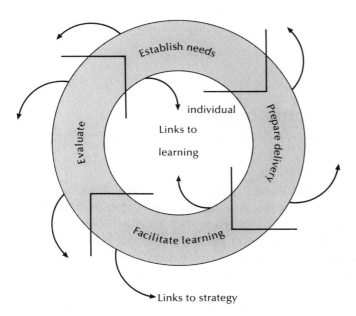

Figure G78.1 The company clutch plate

Glimpse 79
Yorkshire Health's consultants network

In the last few years, Yorkshire Health, previously Yorkshire Regional Health Authority, has worked on a great deal of management and organization development activity in order to support major changes in Health Service provision. Helen Jones, a management and organization development specialist and her colleagues made a deliberate decision not to create an internal full-time unit but instead to recruit independent consultants to help carry out the work.

The consultants' network meets on a regular basis to exchange information and to develop their collective vision of the work. Apart from other business, there is an on-going debate about the identity and purpose of this new, part inside/part outside 'organization'. There seem to be four main ways to think about the group – is it a network, a sub-contracted service, a strategic group or a business?

Elements of all four terms exist. The group is too focused to be a pure network, more involved than a sub-contracted service would imply; the work provides an opportunity to offer strategic help and advice and also to create new business, although it consists mainly of people who are committed elsewhere to running their own businesses. One thing is clear: there is a lot of energy, talent, opportunity and power potential in the consultant's network. Current developments involve product teams and an intention to market products internally and externally to other health authorities, overseas, wherever.

Too clear a definition closes off possibilities. The boundary-spanning nature of the group, developing inside knowledge and expertise with wide outside experience and contacts, makes this a new type of organization with its own managing problems and apparently massive learning and productivity potential.

Glimpse 80
Internal partners

Making PALS – pooling, allying and linking with other businesses – is attractive to a lot of ambitious firms who want to stay small and flexible while developing and growing, but what about those most important partners in your business? You know, the ones you refer to as 'our most valuable asset'.

Lasertek, a small but rapidly expanding specialist engineering concern in southern England, realized that, apart from the three founder directors, everyone else was really just an *employee* – well-paid and highly valued employees, but employees just the same. The directors owned most of the shares and had an interest and commitment the others did not have, yet Lasertek's ambitious plans meant that they must not only *keep* people, but keep them all *growing* in order to take up the opportunities being created. How can people stay and develop with the business and be rewarded for their commitment if their only stake is a weekly wage? Several of the best people were asking this question.

Consultants helped the directors think through the concept of *internal partners* rather than employees. A partner is someone 'who shares' and 'who carries responsibility and risk', they decided. This led to some visioning and brainstorming about the possibilities:

- equity stakes/share options in Lasertek
- franchise opportunities
- 'run your own business in which we'll buy a stake if you wish'
- 'buy your own machine'
- become a managing partner – attend Board meetings and still be a machinist
- set up consultancies
- sell Lasertek part of your time.

The directors decided to investigate these ideas and also to find out what sort of a stake in the business people wanted. Some people might be well content with being well-paid, valued employees; others might want to be partners. The directors soon realized that internal partnerships offered as many growth opportunities as did external ones.

Glimpse 81
Camping on seesaws

In a classic paper, Hedberg, Nystrom and Starbuck suggest six key characteristics likely to equip a company with the capacity to learn in rapidly changing and highly competitive circumstances. To each characteristic they add a choice and thought-provoking aphorism. A Learning Company, they say, needs *minimal* rather than maximal degrees of:

- consensus: 'Cooperation requires minimal consensus'
- contentment about the business: 'Satisfaction rests upon minimal contentment'
- affluence of the business: 'Wealth arises from minimal affluence'
- faith in planning: 'Goals merit minimal faith'
- consistency in linking future with past actions: 'Improvement depends upon minimal consistency'
- rationality in terms of explaining how things happen: 'Wisdom demands minimal rationality'.

So, a complete lack of these characteristics = disorder, but too much of these = complacency. The golden rule is, 'just a little bit more than not enough' of these characteristics provides for frequent triggering, easy unlearning and enough slack to implement new strategies.

REFERENCE

Hedberg, B., P. Nystrom and W. Starbuck, 'Camping on Seesaws: Prescriptions for a Self-designing Organization', *Administrative Science Quarterly*, 21(1), pages 41–65 (1976).

Genichi Taguchi, the TQM specialist, has provided a practical application of an idea that has been known to mathematicians for at least 200 years. Known as the Taguchi Loss Function, the key element of this idea is that quality should be defined in terms of the *loss to society as a whole*, not just in terms of 'our' company.

Thus product or service A is of higher quality than B if the loss or waste or dissatisfaction to society as a whole that arises through producing, selling, using and disposing of A is less than that arising from B. This is a radical thought. First, because it includes not just the losses of manufacturing but also in the obtaining of raw materials, distribution, transportation, use of the product and final disposal. Taguchi's own adherents seem to focus largely on the production/customer interface, but this broader view follows easily from that enlargement of the picture from just our company to everybody, including the environment.

There is another way in which we can take a broader view. The Taguchi approach usually concerns the loss, waste or dissatisfaction that occurs when the output or performance of a physical product differs from its specification. For example, the nominal target diameter for an axle might be 2 mm. According to conventional practice, anything within certain limits, say $+$ or $-$ 0.01 mm, will be considered acceptable and the customer will be satisfied.

From Taguchi's viewpoint however, whenever the *actual* value differs from the *nominal*, then loss occurs. Moreover this loss can be measured as the square of the variation, that is, it multiplies geometrically. So, for example, whatever the total dissatisfaction at, say, 0.01 mm over nominal, then it will be 4 times as great at 0.02 mm, 9 times at 0.03 mm, 16 times at 0.04 and so on (see Figure G82.1).

This assumes that nominal is best, that is, that the customer will be dissatisfied if the actual is greater or less than the nominal. In an engineering situation this is often, but not always, the case. If we now extend this concept to *social* loss, then two other situations may be more likely.

The first of these is known as 'the smaller the better', where the customer ideally wants none of the output at all. This is the case, for example, with noise or noxious

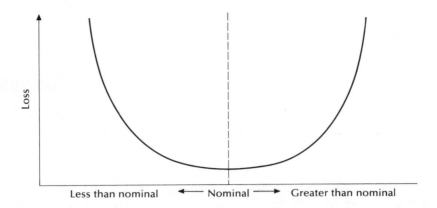

Figure G82.1 The Taguchi loss function

gases or, in the social setting, interpersonal 'noise', such as misunderstandings and unnecessary aggression, or 'social pollution', such as too much stress and tension. Here again, if the loss to everyone rises by the square of the variation, then if stress or tension in our company rises by 10 per cent, the loss to society is 21 per cent (1.1); if it rises by 25 per cent then the loss to society is 56 per cent (see Figure G82.2).

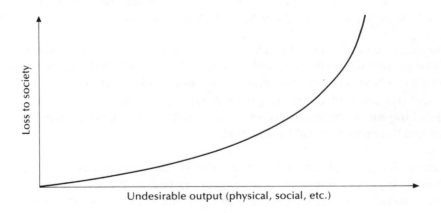

Figure G82.2 Social loss in 'the smaller the better' situation

The converse also applies. By making small reductions in undesirable social outputs, we can make large reductions in the loss to society.

The second source of social loss is in 'the larger the better' situation, where the customer wants as much as possible, for example, in the case of learning.

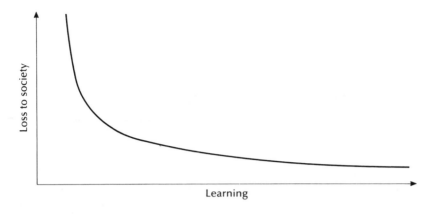

Figure G82.3 Social loss in 'the larger the better' situation

So, increase learning by 10 per cent and you reduce loss geometrically; reduce learning by 10 per cent and the same rule applies to the loss for society – it is far greater than the initial increment.

In engineering we can readily attach numerical or financial values to these graphs. For social scrap it's very difficult to do this, but the principle of the total loss to society and the fact that this varies with the square of the variation, is certainly applicable.

FOLLOW-UP READING

Ealgy, L. A., *Quality by Design: Taguchi Methods and US Industry*, ASI Press (1988).

Glimpse 83
Argyris and Schon on the Learning Company

Of all the theorists on the Learning Company, Chris Argyris and Donald Schon are perhaps the best known. While Reg Revans (see Glimpse 38) seems to focus on the soul of the company, with his emphasis on right relationships, Argyris and Schon are more obviously heirs to the 'brainy' systems tradition. This very brief summary is based on their book *Organizational Learning : A Theory in Action Perspective* (Addison-Wesley, 1978).

Following Gregory Bateson's work, Argyris and Schon suggest that most organizational learning is *single-loop* [O-I] ('error detection and correction') and that there are only isolated examples of *double-loop* [O-II] (learning that changes current operating assumptions, norms and values and which involves deeper inquiry, questioning and, inevitably, conflict and power struggles):

> We have yet to establish, in a full and sustained example, the feasibility of an 0-II organization, nor are we aware of anyone else having done so.

There is also a third variety, *deutero-learning*, that is to do with learning about learning. For Argyris and Schon, organizations can only learn through the agency of individual members and it is through deutero-leraning that the capacity of the whole to learn is brought about:

> When an organization engages in deutero-learning, its members learn, too, about previous contexts for learning. They reflect on and enquire into previous episodes of organizational learning or failure to learn. They discover what they did that facilitated or inhibited learning, they invent new strategies for learning, and they evaluate and generalize what they have produced. The results become encoded in individual maps and images and are reflected in organizational learning practice.

Argyris and Schon's aim is to help organizations to become better at double-loop learning and to learn how to carry out the kinds of enquiry – including the inevitability of conflict – to achieve this. They propose a model of expert-facilitated intervention, combining:

> (a) the mapping of an organization's O-I learning system, (b) helping members of the organization make the transition from model I to model II theories-in-use, (c) guiding and facilitating members' collaborative reflection on and restructuring of, their own learning system, (d) modelling and helping members to model good organizational dialectic in their efforts to detect and correct error in the organization's instrumental theory-in-use.

Glimpse 84
Both . . . and . . . thinking

One of the keys to the Learning Company is thinking differently. Often we are caught in either . . . or . . . thinking – this is either good or bad, possible or impossible. In fact, life can be seen as more various than that, things can often be viewed from more than one point and be both . . . and . . .

A good example in transforming the company is the debate about where to start the change effort. Some people say 'you must start at the top and work downwards'; others that 'you start where there is most chance of success and build on small beginnings'. This is a classic example of the need for both . . . and . . . thinking rather than either . . . or . . .

The Director of a large Social Services Department in a Midlands town said that, after three 'reorganizations' in the last ten years, she had learned that you had to do two things:

> You must give clear direction and then keep up unrelenting pressure for the change from the top *and* you must provide resources, facilities and time to support people whose jobs and lives are affected by the changes. Everyone deserves help and time to work through the individual implications and consequences of organization change.

Now *there's* a useful bit of 'single-loop' learning – next time, she'll do it better – but where's the evidence of 'double-loop' learning here? Has the capacity to be self-transforming been learned during these changes? Could we say that the Social Services Department has an increased capacity to learn, adapt and transform itself as a result of its experience?

That's the ultimate in both . . . and . . . thinking. We can *both* do it better next time *and* we have learned how to learn together.

FOLLOW-UP READING

On both . . . and . . . thinking see Pedler, M., and T. Boydell, *Managing Yourself*, Fontana (1976).

Glimpse 85

Performance-related pay – paying for contributions to the whole

One of the hardest things to do in the Learning Company is to get everyone active, taking individual initiatives and so on, while also being mindful of the whole. To be able to do this, we have to *know* what's going on in the rest of the company, we have to *care* about what happens in the rest of the company and we have to feel able to *contribute* to the whole as well as to improving performance in our own job.

Rewards are important in the Learning Company, and pay is as important here as elsewhere, but the Learning Company pays people to learn and those who join are expected to carry on learning as an implied part of their employment contract. Beyond this, however, the Learning Company also develops the capacity to transform itself, so that, as well as rewarding people for doing their jobs better, it rewards people who make contributions to the whole over and above their own job performance.

This can be built into the normal salary review processes and merit- or performance-related pay given under two headings:

- pay for performance in own job
- pay for contribution over and above own job performance, e.g., for assignment and special project work; for learning new skills useful to the company; for reorganizing work processes; for making successful suggestions; for 'above and beyond' work with customers and so on.

A word of warning. All pay systems degrade over time and in the Learning Company the best systems are those that have been put out to the widest possible consultation. *What* is rewarded under the second heading above, should be agreed by the company as a whole.

Glimpse 86
Gainsharing

People in work expect to get paid well: 'a fair day's pay for a fair day's work' is still an ideal objective for many. In the Learning Company we're asking for greater commitment, for people to keep on learning, to pool that learning with others and to act on the basis of this collective learning in order to transform the business – this calls for more than a hired hand or wage-earner relationship. In consciously linking their own learning and development with that of the company, people are entering into a deeper contract and one that is, essentially, *moral*.

Alan Fox (1974) wrote about this need for a new moral involvement in work in the early 1970s and now is the time of its realization. Pay, of course, is only one aspect of this deeper contract, which must cover rights and obligations of all sorts on both sides, including access to training and development opportunities, a variety of ways of joining, leaving and belonging, etc., that go to making up the new 'partnership' agreement. For the moment, let us stick with pay, the *form* of which – even more than the amount – must acknowledge this new relationship.

Rosabeth Kanter (1989) has recently suggested that there is a trend in the USA away from basic pay increases towards performance pay, profit sharing, employee ownership and gainsharing (a form of profit sharing). She gives as an example the US airline industry, forced to cut costs due to deregulation. Western Airlines, after four years of losses, gave almost a third of the company to its employees, together with two seats on the Board for 10 to 18 per cent wage cuts. Western employees did well on their shares when the company was sold to Delta, but, at Eastern Airlines, where a similar scheme was adopted, the business continued to lose money and employees' stock declined in value, leaving them embittered.

In this example it was 'survival bargaining' that led to more employee partnership. Our own research (1988) suggests that many companies will seek to follow a Learning Company strategy because of increased competition and the need for continuous improvement in order to survive. Other people may have more time, more luck or more foresight. Whatever the conditions, a Learning Company strategy includes finding a way to reward people for being part of something that has been collectively created. The Learning Company, if you like, is shared intellectual, emotional and physical property and the belonging or partnership contract – which replaces the old 'employment contract' – must reflect this.

REFERENCES AND FOLLOW-UP READING

Fox, A., *Beyond Contract*: *Work, Power and Trust Relationships*, Faber & Faber (1974).

Kanter, R.M., *When Giants Learn to Dance*, Simon & Schuster (1989).

Pedler, M. J., J. G. Burgoyne and T. H. Boydell, *Towards the Learning Company*, Final Report to the Training Agency, Moorfoot, Sheffield (May 1988).

Glimpse 87
In praise of dissatisfaction

Although Peters and Waterman have declared (see Glimpse 59) that 'the excellent companies are learning organizations', critics pointed out that a number of their sample seemed to have gone out of their way to disprove the hypothesis in the few years following publication.

There's a paradox here. Perhaps all excellent companies *should* be Learning Companies yet, somehow, 'excellence' proves to be the enemy of learning. People and companies who see themselves as 'excellent' have nothing to learn, no motivation to change, no desire for action. Others call them complacent or say they have lost their drive, vitality or purpose. 'Excellent' people or companies have 'arrived' and, as Abe Maslow said some years ago, 'a satisfied need is no longer a motivator'.

Actually, of course, there usually are plenty of people in 'excellent' companies who are less than happy with what's happening, who are bored, lacking opportunities for development, unhappy with the company products or principles. Often these people do not get a hearing – indeed, often a company is at pains to drown out any criticisms of its managing in a rich and creamy tide of PR.

To see the need for change we must first become dissatisfied. A key task for those who would inspire change is the surfacing and diffusing of dissatisfaction. All revolutionaries know this, but, until recently, it hasn't been a managerial task to go around stirring up dissatisfactions. Now we have it on the impeccable authority of the *Sloan Management Review* that this *is* the job of CEO's – not to be a dissatisfied leader (there are plenty of those), but to be a leader who diffuses dissatisfaction throughout the company, who points it out, who shows how things should be different and who mandates people with less power to start acting to change things.

REFERENCE

Spector, B.A., 'From Bogged Down to Fired Up: Inspiring Organizational Change', *Sloan Management Review*, pages 29–34 (Summer 1989).

Glimpse 88
IBM in the 1990s

Talking of Informating, Christopher O'Malley draws a graphic picture of how IBM will be doing business in the 1990s:

> It is business as usual in 1994: your personal computer, long a tool for individual productivity, is now your window to the resources of the entire company. Clicking on a file-folder icon marked 'US Sales History' quickly connects you to the company's mainframe database, which promptly heeds your request for the background numbers and product photos that will set the stage for your report. Successive clicks on building icons with labels like 'LA' and 'NY' establish invisible links to minicomputer databases in branch offices across the country, enabling you to gather national sales projections and trends as easily as you'd get them from you own spreadsheets. All this information descends neatly into your graphics-based PC, as your minicomputers and mainframe run the same software as you do. Using sophisticated multimedia tools, you combine the collected words, numbers and pictures into an electronic narrative – complete with voice-over – on new market opportunities. You then drag the completed file with an accompanying memo to a phonebook icon, which sends the presentation to company executives across the nation, cueing them to the incoming report via electronic mail.

REFERENCE

O'Malley, C., 'Connecting With Success: IBM Into the Nineties', *Personal Computer Magazine*, VNU Business Publications, page 115 (February 1990).

Glimpse 89
Career evidence

During a conference session at Stratford-upon-Avon, a group of human resource managers went out to the high street to gather some first-hand evidence on 'careers'. Not surprisingly, most of them ended up talking with shop assistants and shop managers, who were usually female.

Most responses showed low expectations and low awareness of the business: 'It's really just a bit of work for money, I don't expect to get much else out of it', said a full-timer with a number of years' service; 'It's just part-time work when they need us, we only find out what's going on from the notices they put up for customers', said another; 'We are having a lot of sales – are we closing or having a new range of products?', queried a third, and added, 'they don't want to know about the problems the customers bring to us'; 'Managers come and go with no apparent reason or explanation', observed an assistant in a well-known chain.

Marks and Spencer were different: assistants were aware of their options – part-time, full-time, becoming a supervisor; supervisors and managers would talk to them about what was involved; staff welfare facilities were in evidence – proper breaks, staffrooms, some taking of personal preferences into account in deciding rosters; training and on-the-job development in new products and procedures happened on a regular basis. It was appreciated.

Some of the human resource managers smelt paternalism, even indoctrination into the party line, yet could not help but feel that here were some basics of good practice that have an important place in the Learning Company.

Glimpse 90
Lapping up the business

Representatives at Mercian Windows have been given lap-top micros that they take with them on sales calls. These have a tailor-made programme that allows the rep to quote immediately for any job by entering the product dimensions and installation conditions.

Before, they either had to guess and take a risk, delve into thick manuals and do a back-of-the-envelope job or go away and prepare a proposal.

Now, they can not only cost a job on the spot, but show a series of alternatives. One drawback that some of them report is that the 'magic box' frightens some of the customers, so it still needs careful handling.

Glimpse 91
The Rover Learning Business

Aware that, as a minnow among whales, it would soon be swallowed up if it stood still, the Rover Car Group launched the Rover Learning Business in May 1990. This £30m business-within-a-business is chaired by Graham Day, Chairman of the Rover Group, and is dedicated to providing learning and development opportunities to all 40 000 members of the Group. All employees can have an individual development plan with the company and the opportunity to learn managing skills.

At the launch conference, the managing director said, 'As a company we desperately needed to learn. We thought there was only one way to run a car manufacturing plant. Our collaboration with Honda taught us differently'. In response to a question, Graham Day said, 'We realize that by encouraging continuous learning and development among all our employees, they will start to question more and more the way we manage things. We will have to learn to respond appropriately to that, but we are not a democracy – the buck stops with management'.

Glimpse 92

The virtuous circle: democracy, profit sharing and information

The Learning Company requires these three values of increased involvement of all its people: a fair sharing of the rewards (or losses) due to the collective effort and free flow of information. Each of these three requires the other two – participation is only possible with full information; full information means that the sharing of rewards has to be seen to be fair; fair shares lead to higher motivation and so on.

A Brazilian machinery manufacturer, Semco, operates on these principles. Semco discovered that size and hierarchy were the main enemies of employee involvement. As a result it has reduced its maximum unit size to about 150 people and reduced the layers of management down to 3. Because managers and management often block what it sets out to facilitate, the titles have been changed – the three layers of management are 'counsellors, partners and coordinators, and everyone else is an 'associate'.

> One of the counsellors and son of the founder, Ricardo Semler, says, . . . that's all there is to it. Participation gives people control of their work, profit sharing gives them a reason to do it better, information tells them what's working and what isn't . . . We are very, very rigorous about numbers. We want them in on the fourth day of the month so that we can have them back by the fifth. And because we're so strict with the financial controls, we can be lax about everything else. Employees can paint the walls any colour they like.

REFERENCE

Semler, R., 'Managing without Managers', *Harvard Business Review*, pages 76–84 (September/ October 1989).

Glimpse 93
We are rich because they are poor . . .

The 'success' and 'excellence' language of recent years has usually meant success or excellence as far as profits are concerned. A few questions will often suffice to show that excellence for shareholders spells something else for others. Some companies realize this, for as well as being financially sound, they reward and develop their employees; have collaborative and mutually beneficial relationships with their suppliers and customers and even act to improve the environments in which they operate. But, even for the best companies, there are still no grounds for the complacency of 'excellence' thinking.

Are you ready for a really stiff question? Then try this.

> What most people in rich countries fail to realize is that their living standards, their empire, involves and requires extensive violence on the part of regimes which force their people to adhere to economic strategies which deprive them and enrich us.
>
> (Trainer 1989)

Surely that's a bit much? Well let's try some real politics

> We have 50% of the world's wealth, but only 6.3% of its population . . . In this situation we cannot fail to be the object of envy and resentment. Our real task in the coming period is to devise a pattern of relationships which will permit us to maintain this position of disparity without positive detriment to our national security.
>
> (George Kennan, Head of US State Department)

Learning Companies try to develop rather than exploit their worlds. There is no end to development, you never finally arrive. Is the 'bottom line' the summit of your corporate ambition? A healthy bottom line could mean that you are now able to widen the horizon and make a different sort of contribution. What could you do to help *develop* rather than exploit that wider world?

REFERENCE AND FOLLOW-UP READING

Trainer, T., *Developed to Death*, Green Print (1989).
Charles, E., 'Is the Price of New Enriched Futures for Some Impoverished Presents for Others?, Paper submitted to the MA in Management Learning at Lancaster University (1990).

Glimpse 94
Assumptions of the times

In Chapter 2 we described how a company moves from the primal through the rational to the integrated phase of its development. The 1970s represented the heyday of the rational approach to learning in organizations (systematic training), whereas in the 1990s we are exploring what an integrated approach might look like.

Each of these two important approaches – systematic training and integrated learning – is based on certain assumptions, some of which are compared in Tables G94.1 and G94.2.

- People are basically passive, dependent, needing extrinsic motivation.
- We can find ways of extrinsically motivating most people, but not everybody.
- People vary with respect to basic abilities and we can measure and remove this variation accurately, predicting job performance accordingly.
- Diversity should therefore be minimized in the interests of order.
- People need to be shown what to do and how to do it (training).
- The output from well-planned training is predictable, constant, with little variation.
- We can measure this performance reliably and consistently.
- Any variation in performance is due almost entirely to the individual.
- Jobs can be broken down into minute parts and then put together again for skilled performance.
- Learning is about changing behaviour in a predictable and constant manner.
- The purpose of one's job is to play one's part in a well-organized, smoothly running structure of interlinked parts.
- The purpose of one's life is not a meaningful concept.
- The whole equals the sum of the parts.
- Cause and effect are closely linked in space and time.
- There are two sets of people and situations: those to whom the above assumptions apply and me.

Table G94.1 Systematic training: some underlying values and assumptions

- People are basically creative, active, intrinsically motivated, and want to do well. Extrinsic motivators at best make no difference, usually make things much worse.
- While people do vary in basic abilities, we should note what they are good at and provide them with jobs that harness this.
- Diversity should therefore be recognized, respected, valued and appreciated in order to bring about creativity and richness in the company.
- People need a wide range of resources and opportunities to enable them to learn established ways and create new ones.
- The output from learning will vary: different people will learn different things in different ways.
- The only way to manage this variety is by providing a great variety of opportunities (Ashby's Law of Requisite Variety).
- It is difficult to measure performance. In any case, we need to provide opportunities for a wide variety of dialogue and feedback, not measurement.
- Variation in performance is almost entirely due to the system, not the individual.
- Jobs cannot be broken into small parts. We need to work on continuous improvement of real outcomes, and issues.
- Learning is about continuous improvement and forever striving to delight my customer.
- The purpose of my job is to delight my customer.
- The purpose of my life is to gain fulfilment by developing to my full potential.
- All too often the whole is less than the sum of the parts. However, it has the potential to be more.
- Cause and effect are widely separated in space and in time.
- These assumptions apply to me and to everyone else.

Table G94.2 Integrated learning: some underlying values and assumptions

FOLLOW-UP READING

Boydell, T.H., *A Guide to Job Analysis*, Bacie (1970).

Deming, W.E., *Out of the Crisis*, Cambridge University Press (1988).

Lessem, R., *Global Management Principles*, Prentice-Hall (1989).

Senge, P., *The Fifth Discipline*, Doubleday/Currency (1990).

Owen, H., *Spirit: Transformation and Development in Organizations*, Abbott Publishing (1987).

Glimpse 95
The evolution of quality

In Chapter 2 we showed how ideas behind training and learning have evolved over the past 35 years or so.

Of course, other fields of specialism have been evolving in a similar way. Indeed, we can take the same archetype of moving through the three phases – primal, rational, integrated – that we used in the earlier chapter and apply it to, for example, the evolution of quality. This is done in Table G95.1; it will be seen that we have used the same P_1, S_1; P_2, S_2, and so on notation as before.

Phase	Date	Problem	Solution
Primal	Mid-nineteenth century.	None (quality is irrelevant).	None needed.
		P_1: we need to stop poor-quality products from leaving the company.	S_1: inspection.
Rational	Invented in the 1930s in USA, but barely adopted there or in UK until 1980s. Adopted in Japan in 1950s.	P_2: inspection is not very effective and costs a lot. Total costs are huge, because of immense expense of scrapping, re-working and so on.	S_2: Statistical Process Control (SPC). Used as a means of spotting errors and poor quality just as they begin to appear, and therefore preventing them from actually occurring.
	1950s Japan, 1980s elsewhere.	P_3: we want to improve not just stabilize things and stop errors.	S_3: SPC as originally intended, i.e., as a means to continuous improvement.
	1950s Japan, 1960s elsewhere.	P_4: (SPC not widely used.) We must aim for zero defects by coordinating the efforts of all our activities.	S_4: Zero Defect Programmes; Quality Assurance; Certification (e.g., BS 5750; ISO 9000).
Integrated	1970s (Japan), 1980s elsewhere.	P_5: 'Just because nothing's wrong doesn't mean everything's right'. People need meaning, purpose and joy in work.	S_5: Total Quality Management (TQM). Deming's 14 points. Win : Win relationships with suppliers and customers. 'Just-in-time' systems.
	1970s Japan, 1980s/ 1990s elsewhere.	P_6: Quality is a moral issue.	S_6: Taguchi – quality as a measure of loss or gain to society at large.

Table G95.1

FOLLOW-UP READING

Deming, W.E., *Out of the Crisis*, Cambridge University Press (1988).
Garvin, D.A., *Managing Quality*, The Free Press (1988).
Neave, H.R., *The Deming Dimension*, SPC Press (1990).

Glimpse 96
Helvig Squares

In this book we have referred often to the need for complementary – both . . . and . . . – rather than simple binary – either . . . or . . . – thinking. Simple advantage seeking can lead to unforeseen disadvantage; overdone strengths become weaknesses and the search for excellence has to be balanced with some complementary humility if it is not to become arrogance.

Helvig (1989) devised an elegant way of putting the phenomenon of complementarity into a graphic form. He stressed that values are always both positive *and* negative and his 'square of values' illustrates what he called their 'polyvalency'. For example, courage is normally thought of as a good quality, but, unless it is balanced by judgement, it becomes foolhardiness (see Figure G96.1):

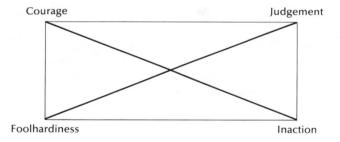

Figure G96.1 A Helvig Square

In Helvig Squares, it is the diagonals that connect opposites, while the two complementary qualities on the top line are only of value when the tension between them is balanced. The bottom line represents the deteriorated or degenerate forms of the positive characteristics. An increase in courage is only of value if it is accompanied by an increase in judgement, otherwise it is in danger of becoming mere foolhardiness.

Imbalance of such qualities is often found in people, but the Helvig Square can also be applied to companies. For example, in the Learning Company there will be *both* a lot of self-development *and* a lot of acting on behalf of and in awareness of the whole company. We can represent these desired qualities as a Helvig Square and reveal the dangers of imbalance (see Figure G96.2):

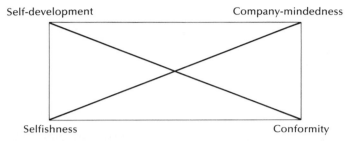

Figure G96.2 A Helvig Square demonstrating need for balance in the Learning Company

Self-development owes much of its current popularity to the need to break out of the stultifying effects of ordered bureaucracy, but if it is not balanced by a sense of membership and ownership of the company, then it will lead to the disintegration of that company.

REFERENCE

Helvig, P., *Charakterologie*, Ernst Klett Verlag (1951).

Glimpse 97
Learning resource centres

Learning resource centres, places where learning packages, resources, aids, help and support are openly accessible in ways that are convenient to users, are clearly good ways to facilitate 'self-development for all' in a Learning Company.

There are many important choices to be made in setting up a learning resource centre. What material/resources? How organized? Should there be diagnostic, that is, need-identifying, help as well as actual learning resources? Should they be just vocational and task-performance oriented or include things oriented to personal development and general education? Should they be places for meeting and discussion among users as well as for using the materials? Should there be human assistance available as well as access to resources? Who should be eligible to use them and how should they be publicized to the potential users? What are the rules about when they can be used – own time or work time?

In practice, learning resource centres often tend to be either like rather flexible little libraries or micro computer labs. We have heard of examples of such centres that are, in practice, not used very much or only by a small minority or, in the extreme, ones that are vandalized.

Designing learning resource centres is probably an art that is still in its infancy, but the concept is a good one.

Glimpse 98
The problem of the ideal company

It is said that there was once a monastery where the monks worked very hard at perfecting the ideal life – presumably in the hope that they could then be a model to the world, which would then instantly follow its example.

The monastery had very thick walls and very closely guarded boundaries, within which the monks searched for their purposes, structures, ways of being. None the less, they fed and drank well – as one should in an ideal society – and the surroundings – outside the walls, supported them in this as in many other things. 'Below stairs' and at the boundaries were people and processes that supported this exchange. They absorbed the difference between the aspiring ideal world and the everyday world of the larger community.

This is both a metaphor and paradox for companies, or parts of companies that seek to perfect themselves and lead by example, practise what they preach and, in the process, deny organization interdependence.

Glimpse 99
The Learning Company – a post-modern phenomenon?

The term 'post-modernism' is perhaps a symptom of itself – a cultural term, much used, with multiple meanings and an implication that the image is all.

In architecture it means a variety of styles and new moves combined as an antithesis to the functional, clear-cut 'modernist' structures. In linguistics and literary criticism it is used to categorize those who recognize that language has a life of its own, independent of any suspect reality to which it refers. In social science it is used to point to, among other things, a world without Utopian direction or clear-cut instrumental goals.

In the world of management and organizational change and development, the modernist tradition can be easily seen. It is the organization development scenario of demolish and/or rebuild around a central purpose, represented in town planning and architecture as demolish, clear, rebuild, start again on a green field site or new town development tradition.

Post-modern organizational change might involve the quest to adapt existing organizations, recognize and build on existing features and strengths – restore rather than re-develop. It may recognize, too, that purposes are unclear, multiple, conflicting. It also brings into focus, but does not resolve, the relationship between a Learning Company that survives and prospers (against some criteria) and a company which is 'good' in some moral, ethical, social responsibility sense, in a world where 'good' is difficult or impossible to define.

Glimpse 100
Reward flexibility

Staff in a large Civil Service department were complaining because a new fast-track management development programme was soaking up all available promotions and demotivating anyone not on the programme. In discussing the department's desire to encourage self-development among all staff, it was clear that the notion of promotion to the next grade as the main reward for learning at work is hopelessly narrow. The logic of the hierarchical pyramid means that most of us will suffer more pain through *not* being promoted than joy when we *are*.

When asked what they wanted in the way of rewards, the staff produced the following list:

- the warmth, support and practical help of colleagues
- opportunities to learn new skills
- performance-related pay
- the right to leave of absence for short periods
- secondments to other departments or to outside companies
- the chance to work flexitime or part-time for spells
- equal opportunities
- workplace nurseries
- a sense of 'running your own business'
- security of employment
- royalties on their ideas
- more flexibility to change jobs
- individual bonuses
- less hierarchy – a sense of being in a good team
- learning and self-development.

In the Learning Company we need to uncouple the association of development with promotion, which has become fixed in our minds. 'Hopping' may replace 'climbing' as the major motivation. Whatever else it does, the Learning Company works hard at legitimizing and rewarding individual and collective learning efforts that are not aimed at promotion. It breaks many of the former taboos surrounding hierarchy, for example, that people 'lower down' earn less than those 'higher up'. Individuals want more control over earnings, just as they do over other aspects of their work, and reward packages in the Learning Company will reflect this.

FOLLOW-UP READING

Kanter, R.M., *When Giants Learn to Dance*, Unwin Hyman (1990).

Glimpse 101
Funny story?

The shop assistant had to disappoint her customer, saying, 'Sorry dear, we don't stock that any more, there's no call for it'.

Then, after pondering for a moment, she said, 'Mind you, people do keep asking for it . . . '

8. Unfinished business

We end this book with the quest started but not finished. We began our search with some of the pioneers who were thinking about the idea of the Learning Company 20 or 30 years ago. We think now that the time, the era and the stage of development that many of our companies have reached mean that we are ready to move in this direction. This book has been written to give you a glimpse of our construction of the Learning Company idea and to provide the encouragement we all need to start big, and possibly risky, journeys.

We intend to continue with our joint research and development work in this field and the rest of this chapter outlines some of our plans and indicates some of the possible problems and directions on which such a search can focus. We hope that some of you will join us in this – perhaps directly, as co-workers; perhaps in spirit, as fellow travellers.

Further research and development work

Some of the problems and difficulties with the idea of the Learning Company need continued and rigorous research. These include the following considerations.

- The whole question of the distribution of power and authority within companies and how the Learning Company idea can come to grips with this, given the various suggestions here, such as, equal access to information, perceived fairness of reward systems and so on
- How will the Learning Company deal with the very knotty problem of rewards, commitment and ownership – in short, the stuff of 'industrial relations'? The Learning Company seems to call for a new involvement in work, it makes use of the 'intellectual property' of all members, so what is, should be, can be the payoffs for all concerned?
- What is the link between the 'good company' (of Glimpse 17 and others) and the Learning Company? There seems to be at least a prima facie case for the Learning Company to be strongly concerned with ecological and ethical issues. P4 (see page 17) is probably concerned with this.
- There seems to us to have been something of a progression in the focus of our concerns about learning in the late twentieth century. We started from the behaviourist and psychoanalytical concerns for learning in the individual. We

have applied learning theories to groups and teams in companies. This book addresses the company as a focus for learning and development. This is new for us personally and perhaps it is new for us as a community of people concerned with improving our individual and collective abilities to manage and organize. Once we can begin to talk sensibly at this level and create data and experience that helps us work here, can the 'Learning *Society*' be far away?

What's next?

Many of the themes and Glimpses in this book point to this wider concern. Once you look outside the Learning Company it is obvious that these collectivities do not exist in isolation. If, for example, the Learning Company calls for perceived fair rewards, an openness in communication and access to information, learning and development for all, is it possible to have this in a society that does not embrace these values? Or, is it true, as we believe, that companies which start to act in these ways have a changing effect on the society of which they are a part?

What we think we can see coming at this societal level is a triangle of forces that constitute the new era (Figure 8.1):

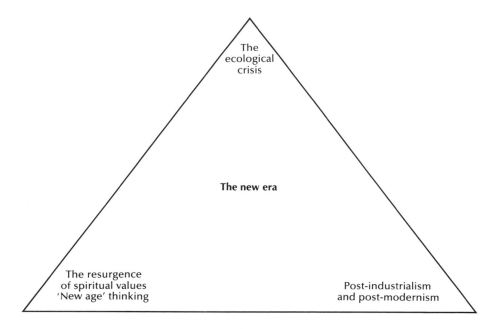

Figure 8.1 The triangle of forces that are forming a new era

There is enough evidence around now to see that we are going to have to learn to cooperate and organize at an unprecedented rate in order to deal with the political and ecological issues that confront us all world-wide. The collective actions that are required not only make a nonsense of existing arrangements for peace and security, but will increasingly require us to change deep-seated beliefs and values concerning sexual and racial characteristics, the fair distribution of the world's wealth, how to develop rather than exploit the environment and so on.

So-called post-modernist thinking challenges our old notions of progress. We have tended to see this in largely material terms. This is especially so in the rich parts of the world, where, ironically, this definition of progress has least validity. The increased valuing of the spiritual dimension of our experience is another link that may indicate in very broad terms where we are going. The challenge of post-modernism and the resurgence of spiritual values, sometimes as evidenced in New Age thinking, seem to be twinned forces out of which the new era will emerge.

How are we going forward?

Returning briefly to earth, our own plans are to try and reconstitute our own learning company – the firm of Pedler, Burgoyne and Boydell that has been practising for the last 15 years – into a new form. We intend to continue working together on the idea of the Learning Company, both in terms of research and also to create tools, resources and design consultancy for those seeking this way forward. If you would like to join us or make a proposal, do get in touch and tell us what you're doing.

AN INVITATION

We hope this book helps you to move towards your own vision of the Learning Company. We are continuing our research and if you are interested you can join us in this process. This is an invitation to respond in two ways:

- *send us your name and address to become part of a Learning Company network* – there are a number of possibilities, such as setting up conferences or a newsletter or simply putting people in touch with each other
- *send us your own Glimpses of the Learning Company* – we chose the word 'Glimpse' because we know that there is no single picture – no blueprint – of the Learning Company (there may be Glimpses of the Learning Company that you have seen but we haven't, so, if you have seen a Glimpse or two of the Learning Company, please send it to us either by post or by fax – we will respect any confidentialities and your intellectual property rights concerning these Glimpses).

We look forward to hearing from you.

TO:

Mike Pedler, John Burgoyne and Tom Boydell,
The Learning Company,
28 Woodholm Road,
Sheffield S11 9HT

Tel/Fax: 0114 2621832

I'd like to offer the following GLIMPSE of the Learning Company:

NAME: TEL. NO;

ADDRESS: FAX: